RESET

RESET

From Broken to Becoming

A 60-Day Journey to Reclaim
Your Peace, Power & Purpose

Charma-Lee Ritchie

Bloom & Ink Legacy Press

Title: Reset From Broken to Becoming

Cover Design: Charma-Lee Ritchie

Published by
Bloom & Ink Legacy Press
ISBN- 979-8234-05957-4

For more resources, visit: www.charmaleeritchie.com

DEDICATION

This book is dedicated to the woman who kept going even when she felt like giving up. To the woman who cried quietly and still showed up for life the next day.

To the woman who trusted, loved, and gave her best, even when it was not returned the way she had hoped. This is for the woman who feels tired in her spirit but still believes that God has more for her.

May these pages wrap around your heart gently. May they remind you that you are not forgotten. May they help you rise again with peace, clarity, and strength.

You are not finished. Your story is still being written. And you are becoming.
"He comforts us in all our troubles, so that we can comfort those in any trouble with the comfort we ourselves receive from God."
— 2 Corinthians 1:4 (NIV)

With love and tenderness,

Charma-Lee Ritchie

NOTE TO THE WOMAN READING

If this book is in your hands, I want you to know this first. You are not alone. Life can break us in ways we never expected. Through loss, disappointment, betrayal, or quiet exhaustion, you may have carried more than anyone knows. But your pain matters, and so does your healing.

This is more than a book. It is a space to breathe. A place where you do not have to pretend or hold everything together. You do not need all the answers. You only need a willing heart and even the smallest seed of faith. God has not forgotten your prayers. He is still able to rebuild what feels broken.

Over the next sixty days, you will gently release what has weighed on you and step into peace, strength, and renewal. There is no rush. Healing is not a race.

You are safe here.

You are seen here.

And you are becoming.

HOW TO USE THIS 60-DAY RESET

This book is a gentle companion for your healing journey. It is not here to overwhelm you. It is here to walk gently beside you. Each day includes a short reading, reflection, prayer, affirmation, and space for you to write. Move at your own pace. Some days you may write deeply. On other days, you may simply read and sit quietly. Both are part of healing.

Create a quiet moment when you open this book. Morning, evening, or any peaceful time will do. There is no perfect schedule. There is only your time.

Write what you truly feel, not what you think you should feel. Healing begins with honesty, and these pages are a safe place for your truth.

At the end of each week, you will find a gentle reset check-in. Pause and notice what is shifting within you. Move through this journey with kindness.

Rest when needed and celebrate small steps forward.
This is your time to reset.
This is your time to heal.
This is your time to become.
Take a deep breath before you begin.
You have carried much, yet you are still here. Over the next sixty days, allow yourself to release what is heavy and receive peace, strength, and renewal. Move gently. Give yourself grace. Your healing begins now.

TABLE OF CONTENTS

PART 2 — THE RESET

Healing • boundaries • spiritual realignment

PART 3 — BECOMING

Confidence • identity • new life

A GENTLE NOTE ABOUT YOUR HEALING JOURNEY

This book is a companion for your heart and spirit as you move through a season of healing and renewal. It is written with care, faith, and tenderness for women who are walking through emotional pain, transition, and personal rebuilding. As you journey through these pages, please remember that healing is not a straight path. Some days you may feel strong and hopeful. Other days you may feel tender or tired. Both experiences are a natural part of the healing process. Move at a pace that feels right for you. There is no pressure to complete each day perfectly or on a strict schedule. What matters most is your willingness to show up for yourself with honesty and grace.

This book offers encouragement, reflection, and spiritual support. It is not a substitute for professional medical, psychological, or therapeutic care. If you are experiencing deep emotional distress or find that past wounds feel overwhelming, seeking support from a qualified counselor, therapist, or trusted spiritual advisor can be a wise and loving step toward your well-being.

Be gentle with yourself as you read and write. Allow these pages to be a safe place where you can release what has been heavy and receive what brings peace. Your healing matters. Your heart matters. And you deserve care, patience, and compassion as you move forward.
Take this journey one day at a time, trusting that even small steps can lead to meaningful transformation.

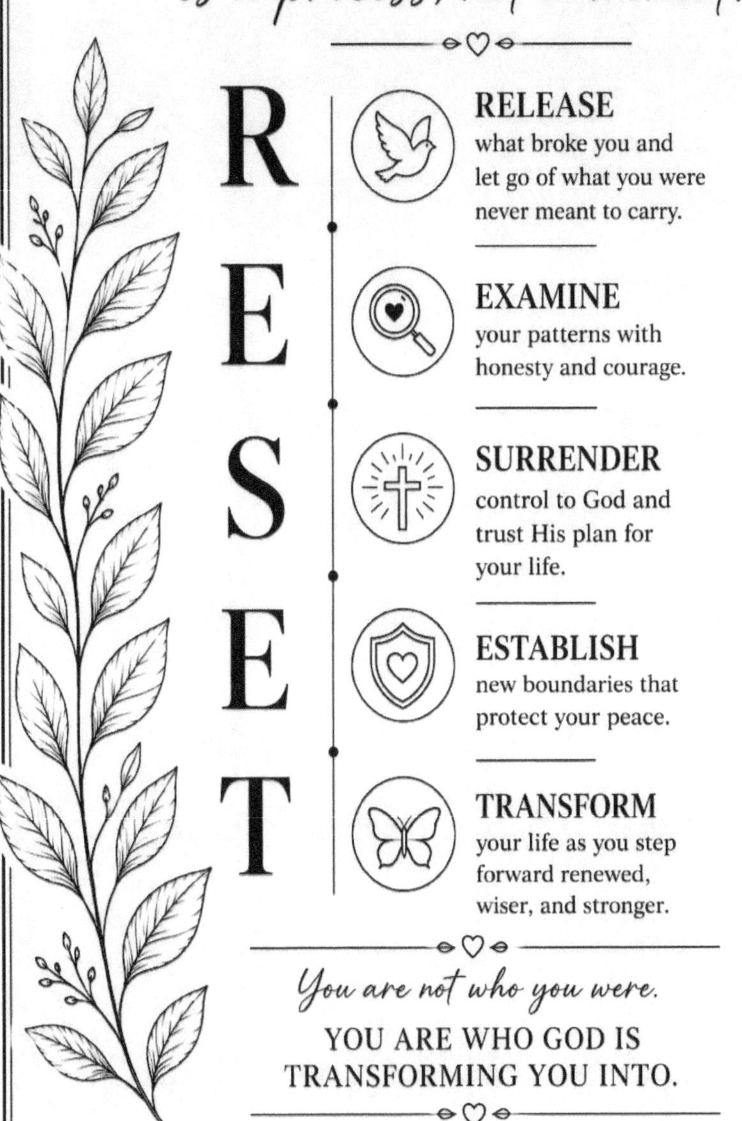

R.E.S.E.T.

is a process, not a moment.

R

RELEASE
what broke you and
let go of what you were
never meant to carry.

E

EXAMINE
your patterns with
honesty and courage.

S

SURRENDER
control to God and
trust His plan for
your life.

E

ESTABLISH
new boundaries that
protect your peace.

T

TRANSFORM
your life as you step
forward renewed,
wiser, and stronger.

You are not who you were.

YOU ARE WHO GOD IS
TRANSFORMING YOU INTO.

PART ONE

THE BREAKING

Release. Honesty. Emotional Truth.

Day 1

When Life Breaks in Unexpected Places

There are moments in life that arrive without warning. One day, you are moving forward with plans and expectations, and the next, you find yourself standing in a reality you never imagined for your life. It can feel disorienting when what once felt secure begins to shift beneath your feet. You may wonder how things changed so quickly or why certain experiences found their way into your story.

When life breaks in unexpected places, it often leaves us searching for stability. The heart tries to make sense of what it cannot fully understand. Questions arise that do not always have immediate answers. In those moments, it is easy to feel alone, even when others are around you. Yet within that quiet space, God remains present. He is not startled by the turns your life has taken. He is not distant from your pain. He is aware of every moment that has brought you to this day.

It is important to allow yourself to acknowledge what has happened without minimizing your feelings. Strength does not come from pretending that you are untouched by hardship. True strength begins when you allow yourself to be honest about what you are carrying. Today is not about fixing everything at once. Today is about gently recognizing where you are and allowing grace to meet you there. His word declares in Psalm 147:3, "He heals the brokenhearted and binds up their wounds."

Even in unexpected breaking, there is still a path forward. There is still purpose ahead of you. There is still healing that can unfold in ways you may not yet see. God has a way of meeting us in the very places we feel most fragile and reminding us that our lives are not defined by what has been broken, but by what can be restored. Let this be the beginning of a gentle return to yourself. You are allowed to feel. You are allowed to pause. You are allowed to begin again, even from here.

Healing Reflection

What unexpected change or experience has most affected your heart, and how has it shaped how you feel today?

Reset Prayer

Loving Heavenly Father,

You see every part of my life and every place where I feel broken or uncertain. Nothing about my story is hidden from You. Today, I bring my heart before You just as it is. Where I'm confused, please bring clarity. Where I feel pain, bring comfort. Where I feel weak, bring strength. Help me to trust that even in unexpected moments, You are still guiding my life. Hold me gently as I begin this journey of healing and renewal. Amen.

Affirmation

I am not defined by what has broken. With God's help, I am being gently restored.

Your Reflection Space

Day 2

Admitting I Am Not Okay

There are times in life when we try to remain strong for everyone around us. We carry responsibilities, expectations, and quiet pressures that tell us to keep going even when our hearts feel heavy. We smile when we are hurting and continue moving forward even when we feel exhausted inside. Over time, this quiet strength can become a burden when we do not allow ourselves the space to acknowledge how we truly feel.

Admitting that you are not okay does not mean you are weak. It means you are honest. There is a quiet courage in facing your emotions without hiding from them. Many women have learned to push through pain without pausing to care for their own hearts. Yet healing begins the moment we stop pretending and start telling the truth, even if that truth is spoken softly in prayer.

God does not ask you to appear strong before Him. He already sees what you carry. He understands the weight of your thoughts and the depth of your emotions. When you come before Him honestly, without masks or defenses, you open the door for comfort and restoration to begin. There is no shame in acknowledging that you feel tired, overwhelmed, or uncertain. Your honesty becomes the first step toward peace. Scripture says in 2 Corinthians 12:9, "My grace is sufficient for you, for My power is made perfect in weakness."

Today is an invitation to release the pressure to have everything together. You are allowed to pause and admit what you feel without judgment. You are allowed to acknowledge the places where you need healing and support. In that gentle honesty, something within you begins to soften. In that honesty, God meets you with compassion rather than condemnation.

Let today be a moment of truth, spoken with kindness toward yourself. You do not have to carry everything alone. You do not have to hide your emotions. You can bring your whole heart before God and trust that He receives you with understanding and love.

Healing Reflection

In what areas of your life have you been pretending to be strong when you are actually feeling overwhelmed or weary?

Reset Prayer

Heavenly Father,
You know me completely and understand every emotion I carry. Today, I come before You without pretending. Where I feel overwhelmed, bring me peace. Where I feel tired, give me rest. Where I feel uncertain, reassure me. Help me to be honest with myself and with You. Teach me that I do not have to hide my struggles to be loved and supported. Hold my heart gently as I learn to release what I have been carrying alone. Amen.

Affirmation

I release the need to appear strong. In honesty and faith, I am being gently restored.

Your Reflection Space

Day 3

The Weight I Have Been Carrying

There are burdens we carry that no one else can see. They sit quietly in the heart and mind, growing heavier over time. Responsibilities, disappointments, unspoken fears, and past wounds can slowly gather until we feel weighed down without fully understanding why. Sometimes we become so accustomed to carrying these things that we forget what it feels like to move through life with lightness and peace.

You may have learned to carry more than your share. You may have taken on the emotional weight of others while quietly setting aside your own needs. You may have held together situations that felt as though they were falling apart. In doing so, you showed strength and endurance. Yet even the strongest heart needs moments of rest and release. No one was created to carry every burden alone.

God never intended for you to hold everything by yourself. He understands the pressures you have faced and the silent struggles you have endured. When life feels heavy, it is often an invitation to come closer to Him and allow Him to share the weight. You do not have to explain everything perfectly. You do not have to find the right words. Simply bringing your honest heart before Him is enough.

Today is a gentle reminder that you are allowed to set down what has become too heavy. You are allowed to release what no longer belongs in your hands. There is relief in acknowledging that you cannot carry everything and that you were never meant to. As you begin to release what has been weighing on you, you create space for peace to enter and remain.

Let this be a day of gentle release. Not all at once, but little by little. Each time you let go of a worry, a fear, or a lingering hurt, you create space for healing. Each time you trust God to carry what you cannot, your spirit grows lighter. You were never meant to bear it all. You deserve to move forward free from the weight that was never yours to hold.

Healing Reflection

What emotional weight or hidden burden have you been carrying that you are ready to begin releasing?

Reset Prayer

Gracious Father,
You see every burden I've been carrying and the weight upon my heart. Today, I lay it all before You with confidence. Where I have felt overwhelmed, You are bringing relief. Where pressure has weighed on me, You are establishing Your peace.

I release what is not mine to control, trusting fully that You can carry what I cannot. You are my strength, my covering, and my rest. Teach me to remain anchored in Your care, steady and unshaken, as I move forward lighter, freer, and renewed.
Thank You for walking beside me, for holding me with tenderness, and for restoring my soul as I heal.
Amen.

Affirmation

I am no longer carrying everything alone. With God's help, I am releasing what is too heavy for me.

Your Reflection Space

Day 4

When Trust Is Shattered

Trust is a delicate part of the heart. It is built slowly over time through love, honesty, and consistency. When trust is honored, it creates safety and connection. When trust is broken, it can leave deep wounds that are not always visible to others. The pain of shattered trust can cause you to question not only others but also yourself and the future you once believed in.

When trust is broken, it often leaves behind confusion and sadness. You may find yourself wondering how things changed or why certain events unfolded the way they did. It is natural to replay moments in your mind, searching for understanding. Yet not every question has a clear answer. Some wounds require time and gentle care rather than immediate resolution.

God understands the pain that comes when trust is shattered. He sees the moments that caused your heart to close and the disappointment that followed. He does not rush you to move on or expect you to pretend that nothing happened. Instead, He meets you with a steady, unfailing presence. While people may falter, God remains constant and faithful. His love is not fragile, and His care for you never wavers.

Healing from broken trust does not happen overnight. It is a gradual process that begins with acknowledging the hurt rather than burying it. You are allowed to feel what you feel without judgment. You are allowed to take time to heal without pressure.

As you move forward, God can gently rebuild your sense of safety and help you learn to trust again, first in Him and then, when you are ready, in others who prove themselves worthy of that trust.

Today is not about forcing yourself to trust again quickly. It is about allowing God to hold the pieces of your heart with care. In His hands, what feels shattered can slowly be restored. In His presence, you can find a steady place where trust begins again, not in fear but in quiet confidence that you are never alone.

Healing Reflection

How has broken trust affected your heart, and what emotions surface when you think about trusting again?

Reset Prayer

Faithful God,

You see the places where my trust has been broken and the pain that remains. You understand the disappointment and confusion that I carry. Today, I bring my wounded heart to You. Comfort me where I feel hurt. Restore me where I feel fragile. Help me to trust Your steady presence even when I feel uncertain about others. Teach me that I am safe in Your care and that healing is possible for my heart. Walk with me gently as You rebuild what has been damaged within me. Amen.

Affirmation

My heart is held safely by God. In His care, trust can be restored.

Your Reflection Space

Day 5

Grieving What I Thought My Life Would Be

There is a quiet grief that comes when life does not unfold the way we imagined. It is the sorrow of unmet expectations, broken plans, and dreams that once felt certain. Sometimes this grief is difficult to explain because nothing visible may have ended, yet something inside feels lost. You may find yourself mourning the life you thought you would have, the love you believed would last, or the peace you expected to feel by now.

Grieving what could have been a deeply human experience. It does not mean you lack faith. It does not mean you are ungrateful for what you still have. It simply means your heart is acknowledging a loss that mattered to you. There is no shame in admitting that you hoped for something different. There is no weakness in feeling sadness over the life you once envisioned.

God understands this kind of grief. He sees the silent disappointments and the private tears that come when reality feels different from what you prayed for. He does not dismiss your feelings or ask you to ignore them. Instead, He invites you to bring your honest heart to Him. In His presence, you can release what you thought your life would be and slowly begin to accept what is unfolding now. His word says in Joel 2:25 "I will restore to you the years that the locust has eaten."

Letting go of an imagined future is not easy, but it creates space for a new beginning. When you release what no longer exists, you make room for what is still possible.

God can shape beauty out of unexpected paths and create purpose in places you never planned to walk. Even now, He is gently guiding you toward a future that can still hold peace, meaning, and joy.

Today is a day to acknowledge what you are grieving without judgment. Allow yourself to feel it fully, then place it in God's hands. In time, what feels like loss can become the soil where new hope quietly begins to grow.

Healing Reflection

What expectations, plans, or dreams have you been grieving, and how have they affected the way you see your life right now?

Reset Prayer

Compassionate Father,
You know the dreams I once held and the life I thought I would be living. You see the disappointment and quiet grief within my heart. Today I bring these feelings to You with honesty. Comfort me where I feel loss. Strengthen me where I feel uncertain. Help me release what can no longer be and trust that You are still leading me toward a meaningful and peaceful future. Restore hope within me and guide my steps with Your gentle wisdom. Amen.

Affirmation

I release the life I once imagined and open my heart to the peace and purpose still ahead of me.

Your Reflection Space

Day 6

Silent Tears God Still Sees

Some tears fall where no one else can see them. Even in the quiet moments when you appear strong on the outside, I acknowledge the tenderness within, and I stand steady, unshaken.

You may move through your day fulfilling responsibilities, offering kindness, and showing strength, yet inside, there is a tenderness that longs to be acknowledged. Silent tears often carry the emotions we struggle to express aloud. They hold grief, disappointment, and the quiet weight of everything we have endured. The bible says in Psalm 56:8, "You keep track of all my sorrows. You have collected all my tears in Your bottle. You have recorded each one in Your book."

Even when no one else notices these tears, God sees each one. He is present in the moments when you feel most alone and understands the language of your heart without you having to explain every detail. Nothing about your pain is hidden from Him. Every sigh, every moment of heaviness, and every silent cry is known and gently held by His compassionate presence.

Sometimes we try to hide our tears because we feel we must remain strong. We may believe that expressing our pain will burden others or make us appear weak. Yet there is strength in allowing yourself to feel and release what has been building within you. Tears are not a sign of failure. They are often the beginning of healing. When you allow yourself to feel honestly, your heart begins to soften and open to comfort and restoration.

Today is a reminder that you do not have to hide your emotions from God. You can bring your silent tears into His presence without fear or shame. He receives them with tenderness and understanding. In His care, those tears are not wasted. They become part of the healing process that slowly restores your peace and renews your strength.

Let this be a day where you allow yourself to feel without judgment. You are not alone in your quiet moments. God is near, holding you with compassion and guiding you gently toward healing.

Healing Reflection

What emotions or struggles have you been holding inside that you have not expressed openly to anyone?

Reset Prayer

Loving Father,
You see every tear I have cried, even the ones no one else knows about. You understand the emotions I carry and the places where I feel fragile. Today, I bring my silent tears to You. Comfort my heart and remind me that I am never alone. Help me to release what I have been holding inside and to trust that You are gently healing me. Surround me with Your peace and renew my strength as I continue this journey. Amen.

Affirmation

God sees every tear I have cried. I am held in His compassion and gently being restored.

Your Reflection Space

Day 7

I Gave So Much and Lost Myself

There are seasons in life when you give from a sincere and loving place. You give your time, your care, your patience, and your support. You show up for others when they need you and offer your strength even when you feel tired. Giving is a beautiful part of who you are. Yet there are times when giving without balance can leave you feeling empty and disconnected from yourself.

You may look back and realize that somewhere along the way, you began to neglect your own needs. You poured into others while quietly setting aside your own desires, rest, and emotional well-being. Over time, this can create a deep weariness. It can feel as though you have given so much that there is little left for yourself. In those moments, it is easy to wonder how you arrived at this place and how you can begin to find yourself again. Psalm 23:3 "He restores my soul."

God sees every act of love you have offered. He sees the sacrifices you made and the ways you tried to hold things together. Nothing you gave with a sincere heart has been wasted or unseen. At the same time, God does not ask you to lose yourself to love others. He desires wholeness for you. He desires that you live with peace, strength, and a clear sense of who you are.

Finding yourself again begins with gentle awareness. It begins by recognizing that your needs matter too. You are allowed to rest. You are allowed to rediscover what brings you peace and joy.

You are allowed to care for your own heart with the same kindness you have shown others. This is not selfish. It is necessary for healing and renewal. Today is an invitation to begin returning to yourself. Not all at once, but step by step. As you acknowledge where you feel depleted, you create space for restoration. As you choose to honor your own well-being, you move closer to balance and peace. You have given much, but you are not lost.

The woman you are is still present and worthy of care. Allow yourself to move forward with compassion toward your own heart. You deserve to feel whole again. You deserve to feel present in your own life. With God's guidance, you can rediscover who you are and step into a season where giving and receiving flow in gentle harmony.

Healing Reflection

In what ways have you given so much of yourself that you began to feel disconnected from your own needs and identity?

Reset Prayer

Gracious Father,

You know the ways I have poured into others and the places where I now feel empty or tired. Thank You for the heart You gave me to love and care deeply. Today I ask for restoration. Help me to rediscover who I am and to care for myself with wisdom and balance. Teach me that honoring my own well-being is not selfish but necessary. Renew my strength and guide me as I begin to return to myself with gentleness and grace. Amen.

Affirmation

I am rediscovering myself with compassion. I deserve balance, peace, and renewal.

Your Reflection Space

Day 8

The Loneliness No One Notices

There is a quiet kind of loneliness that can linger, even in the midst of a crowd. It is the quiet feeling of being unseen, unheard, or misunderstood. You may carry on with daily responsibilities, conversations,
and interactions, while inside you feel a distance that is difficult to explain. This type of loneliness does not always come from being physically alone. It often comes from feeling emotionally disconnected or unsupported in ways that matter deeply.

You may have learned to hide this loneliness behind strength and routine. You show up for others, offer kindness, and continue fulfilling what is expected of you. Yet there are moments when you long for someone to truly understand your heart without you having to explain everything. You may wish for comfort that reaches beyond surface conversations and touches the deeper places within you.

God sees the loneliness that others may not notice. He understands the quiet spaces where you feel alone and the unspoken thoughts you carry. Even when it seems that no one fully understands your journey, God remains present and attentive. His care for you does not depend on how visible your pain is to others. He is always nearby, providing a steady presence that never fades.

Acknowledging your loneliness is not a sign of weakness; it is an act of honesty and courage. When you allow yourself to confront what you truly feel, you create space for genuine connection and healing to begin.

Today can be a gentle step forward, inviting God into the places that feel empty, trusting that He will meet you there with presence, comfort, and quiet restoration. His presence reaches into places of quiet isolation, bringing deep comfort and gently reminding you that you are never truly alone.

Let this be a day of gentle awareness. Notice what you feel without judging it. Allow yourself to bring that loneliness into prayer rather than carrying it silently. In doing so, you create room for peace and reassurance to settle into your heart. Even in moments when others may not see you fully, God sees you completely and holds you with care.

Healing Reflection

When do you feel most alone or unseen, and what do you long for in those moments?

Reset Prayer

Loving Father,
You know the moments when I feel alone and the places where I feel unseen. Thank You for being present even when I struggle to feel it. Today I bring my loneliness before You. Fill the empty spaces within my heart with Your peace and comfort. Remind me that I am never forgotten and never alone. Draw me into a deeper awareness of Your presence, and strengthen my trust that You are walking with me each day. Amen.

Affirmation

I am never truly alone. God sees me, understands me, and walks with me always.

Your Reflection Space

Day 9

When Love Hurts Instead of Heals

Love is meant to bring comfort, safety, and connection. It is meant to nurture the heart and create a sense of belonging. Yet there are times when love becomes a source of pain rather than peace. When this happens, it can leave deep confusion within the heart. You may find yourself questioning what went wrong or wondering why something that began with hope now feels heavy and wounded.

Experiencing hurt within relationships can be one of the most difficult forms of pain to process. When you open your heart, you do so with trust and sincerity. You invest emotionally and spiritually, hoping for mutual care and understanding. When that care is not returned as you hoped, the disappointment can cut deeply. It can unsettle your sense of safety and leave you uncertain about how to move forward.

God understands the pain that comes when love wounds rather than heals. He sees the sincerity of your heart and the depth of your desire to give and receive genuine love. He does not dismiss your feelings or ask you to ignore them. Instead, He offers a steady presence that brings comfort and clarity. In His care, you can begin to sort through what has hurt you and what you truly need for your well-being.

It is important to remember that experiencing pain in love does not mean you are unworthy of healthy and nurturing relationships. It does not mean that love itself is meant to harm you. It simply means that healing and discernment are needed.

When you allow God to guide your heart, you begin to recognize what true, supportive love looks like and how to protect your emotional and spiritual well-being.

Today is a day to acknowledge any hurt you have experienced in love without self-blame or shame. You are allowed to feel what you feel. You are allowed to seek healing and peace. As you bring your wounded places to God, He can gently restore your heart and help you move forward with greater wisdom and strength.

Healing Reflection

How have past or present relationships affected your ability to feel safe, valued, and loved?

Reset Prayer

Faithful Father,

You see the places where my heart has been hurt and the ways I have struggled to understand love. Today I bring these experiences to You. Comfort me where I feel wounded. Heal the parts of my heart that feel fragile or uncertain. Help me to recognize the kind of love that brings peace and supports my well-being. Guide me as I move forward with wisdom, strength, and renewed trust in Your care. Amen.

Affirmation

I am worthy of love that brings peace, respect, and healing to my life.

Your Reflection Space

Day 10

Releasing the Need for Answers

There are moments in life when questions seem to linger without resolution. You may find yourself wondering why certain things happened, why people acted the way they did, or why your path has taken unexpected turns. The heart naturally seeks understanding because answers can feel like a form of closure. Yet not every question receives a clear response, and not every situation can be fully explained.

Holding onto the need for answers can sometimes keep you tied to pain. When the mind continuously searches for explanations, it can become difficult to find peace in the present moment. You may feel stuck between what has happened and what you wish you could understand. This inner tension can quietly drain your emotional energy and prevent you from moving forward with ease.

God understands your desire for clarity. He knows that unanswered questions can feel heavy and unsettling. At the same time, He gently reminds you that peace does not always come from knowing every detail. Sometimes peace comes from trusting that even without full understanding, your life is still held in His care. He sees the complete picture, including the parts that remain hidden from you.

Releasing the need for answers does not mean ignoring what you have experienced. It means allowing yourself to rest in the truth that you do not need to understand everything to heal.

You can choose peace even when questions remain. You can choose to focus on what is before you rather than what cannot be changed. This release creates space for emotional freedom and spiritual renewal. Proverbs 3:5–6 "Trust in the Lord with all your heart and lean not on your own understanding; in all your ways submit to Him, and He will make your paths straight."

Today is your invitation to loosen your grip on unanswered questions and rest in the peace of not having to carry them. You do not have to carry them endlessly. You can place them in God's hands and trust that He is guiding your life with wisdom and care. As you release the need to understand everything, you may begin to feel a gentle lightness returning to your heart.

Healing Reflection

What questions or situations have you been holding onto that continue to weigh on your mind and heart?

Reset Prayer

Heavenly Father,
You know the questions I carry and the answers I wish I had. Today, I release my need to understand everything. Help me to trust that You see what I cannot and that You are guiding my life with wisdom and love. Replace my restless thoughts with Your peace. Teach me to rest in Your care even when I do not have all the answers. Strengthen my heart as I choose trust over worry and peace over confusion. Amen.

Affirmation

I release the need for every answer. I choose peace and trust in God's care.

Your Reflection Space

Day 11

Facing What I Tried to Avoid

There are experiences and emotions that we sometimes try to set aside because they feel too heavy to confront. We tell ourselves that if we stay busy, remain strong, or focus on moving forward, the discomfort will fade on its own. Avoidance can feel like protection in the moment. It can seem easier to look away from what hurts rather than sit with it honestly. Yet over time, what we avoid often remains quietly present within us.

Avoiding pain does not make it disappear. It simply waits for a moment when it can be acknowledged and understood. You may have avoided certain memories, conversations, or emotions because they felt overwhelming. You may have hoped that time alone would resolve everything. While time can soften wounds, true healing often begins when we gently face what we have tried to push aside.

God meets you with compassion as you begin to face what has been difficult. He does not approach your heart with judgment or pressure. Instead, He offers a steady presence and the reassurance that you do not have to confront anything alone. What once felt too painful to acknowledge can become manageable when you bring it into His care. With His guidance, you can begin to look at your experiences with honesty and without fear.

Facing what you have avoided is not about reliving pain or placing blame. It is about creating space for understanding and release.

When you allow yourself to acknowledge what has been hidden, you take a meaningful step toward freedom. You begin to loosen the hold that unresolved emotions may have had on your thoughts and spirit. Each moment of honest reflection becomes a step toward greater peace.

Today is your invitation to gently turn toward what you have been avoiding, with courage, honesty, and grace. You do not need to rush or force anything. Move at a pace that feels safe and steady. With God beside you, you can look at your experiences with courage and compassion. What once felt too difficult to face can become the very place where healing begins.

Healing Reflection

Is there a memory, emotion, or situation you have been avoiding that may need gentle acknowledgment and release?

Reset Prayer

Compassionate Father,
You know the parts of my life I have tried to avoid and the emotions I have struggled to face. Today I ask for Your courage and comfort. Help me to gently acknowledge what I have been carrying without fear or shame. Walk with me as I face what has been difficult and bring healing to the places that need Your touch. Thank You for guiding me with patience and love as I move toward freedom and peace. Amen.

Affirmation

With God beside me, I face my truth gently and move toward healing and peace.

Your Reflection Space

Day 12

My Heart Is Tired

There are seasons when weariness settles deep within the heart. It is not always visible to others, yet you feel it in quiet moments. You may continue to meet responsibilities and care for those around you while carrying an inner exhaustion that is difficult to explain. Emotional fatigue can come from giving too much, holding too much, or enduring too much without enough time to rest and recover.

A tired heart does not mean you are weak. It often means you have been strong for a long time. You have carried responsibilities, managed disappointments, and kept moving forward even when you felt drained. Over time, this constant effort can leave you feeling depleted. You may feel your energy fade, a quiet heaviness settle in, and a growing desire to withdraw and deeply rest. These feelings are signals from your heart that it needs gentleness and care.

God understands the weariness you feel. He sees every effort you have made and every moment you pushed forward despite feeling tired. He does not expect you to continue without rest. Instead, He invites you into His presence where you can find renewal and peace. When you bring your exhaustion to Him, you are not admitting defeat. You are acknowledging your need for restoration and allowing Him to strengthen you. Matthew 11:28–30 (NIV) "Come to me, all you who are weary and burdened, and I will give you rest. Take my yoke upon you and learn from me, for I am gentle and humble in heart, and you will find rest for your souls. For my yoke is easy and my burden is light."

Rest for the heart begins with permission. Permission to pause. Permission to breathe. Permission to acknowledge that you cannot pour endlessly without receiving care in return. Today can be a gentle moment of stillness where you allow yourself to release the pressure to keep going at the same pace. In that pause, you may begin to feel a quiet renewal taking place within you.

Let this day be one of compassion toward yourself. You do not have to carry everything at once. You do not have to force strength when you need rest. As you allow your heart to slow down and receive care, healing begins in subtle and meaningful ways. A rested heart can find hope again. A cared-for heart can begin to feel light once more.

Healing Reflection

In what ways has your heart been feeling tired, and what kind of rest or support do you feel you need right now?

Reset Prayer

Gentle and Loving Father,
You see the weariness in my heart and the moments when I feel emotionally exhausted. Today, I come to You seeking rest and renewal. Help me to release the pressure to keep pushing forward without caring for myself. Restore my strength and bring peace to my spirit. Teach me to rest in Your presence and to trust that I am supported and sustained by Your love. Thank You for renewing me gently and faithfully. Amen.

Affirmation

I permit myself to rest. My heart is being renewed with peace and gentle strength.

Your Reflection Space

Day 13

The Fear of Starting Over

Starting over can feel both necessary and overwhelming. There are moments when life shifts in ways you did not plan, and you find yourself standing at the beginning of something new without the comfort of familiarity. Even when you know that change is needed, the uncertainty of what lies ahead can create fear. You may wonder if you have the strength to rebuild or if you will find stability and peace again.

The fear of starting over often comes from what you have already experienced. When you have faced disappointment, loss, or emotional pain, the idea of beginning again can feel risky. You may hesitate to hope too deeply or trust too quickly. Part of you may long for a fresh start, while another part feels unsure about stepping forward. These mixed emotions are natural. They reflect both your desire for healing and your need for reassurance.

God recognizes the vulnerability that accompanies new beginnings. He understands the courage needed to let go of the familiar and embrace the unknown. Even when the path ahead feels uncertain, you are not walking alone. God moves with you, guiding each step with wisdom and care. He does not expect you to have everything figured out. He invites you to trust that He can guide you towards a future that is filled with purpose and peace.

Starting over does not mean you are losing everything. It often means you are making room for growth, clarity, and renewal. Each new step carries the possibility of healing and discovery.

You bring with you the lessons you have learned and the strength you have gained. These become the foundation for what you are building now. What once felt like an ending can slowly become the beginning of something meaningful and steady.

Today is an invitation to acknowledge any fear you feel about starting again. Rather than pushing it away, hold it gently and bring it into prayer. Allow yourself to imagine a future that holds stability and hope. With God's presence guiding you, new beginnings can become less frightening and more filled with possibility. You are not stepping into the unknown without support. You are stepping forward with faith and quiet courage.

Healing Reflection

What fears or uncertainties arise when you think about starting over or entering a new season in your life?

Reset Prayer

Faithful Father,
You know the fears that surface when I think about beginning again. You see the uncertainty I feel and the questions that fill my mind. Today, I place my fears in Your hands. Replace anxiety with peace and doubt with trust. Help me to believe that new beginnings can lead to healing and growth. Walk beside me as I move forward and remind me that I am never alone. Thank You for guiding me with wisdom and compassion as I step into this new season. Amen.

Affirmation

I move forward with quiet courage. With God beside me, new beginnings are filled with hope and purpose.

Your Reflection Space

Day 14

Letting God into the Pain

There are moments when pain settles deep within the heart and feels difficult to share. You may carry emotions that are hard to put into words or experiences that feel too personal to express. Sometimes it can seem easier to keep these feelings inside rather than open them to anyone else. Yet the weight of unspoken pain can quietly grow heavier when it is carried alone.

Letting God into your pain is not about having perfect words or a complete understanding. It is about allowing yourself to be honest in His presence. God already sees what you feel and understands what you have endured. He does not turn away from your sorrow or ask you to hide it. Instead, He invites you to bring every part of your heart to Him, including the places that feel most tender and vulnerable.

When you allow God into your pain, you create space for comfort and healing to begin. You no longer have to carry everything alone or pretend that you are unaffected. You can come before Him with your questions, your sadness, and your uncertainty. In His presence, you are met with compassion rather than judgment. He listens with patience and responds with a peace that gently settles within you.

Opening your heart to God may feel unfamiliar at first, especially if you have grown used to handling everything on your own. Yet each time you choose to share your true feelings with Him, you take a step toward healing.

You allow His presence to meet you where you are and to bring light into places that once felt heavy. Over time, this openness creates a deeper sense of trust and connection.

Today is an invitation to let God into the places that hurt. You do not need to hide your tears or guard your emotions. Speak honestly, even if your words feel simple or uncertain. In doing so, you allow His comfort to reach the deepest parts of your heart. Healing often begins in these quiet moments of openness and trust.

Healing Reflection

What pain or emotion have you been holding inside that you may be ready to bring honestly before God today?

Reset Prayer

Loving Father,

You know every part of my heart and every place where I feel pain. Today, I open my heart to You without hiding anything. Receive my sorrow, my questions, and my fears with Your compassion. Bring comfort where I feel wounded and peace where I feel troubled. Help me to trust that I can bring everything to You and be met with understanding and care. Thank You for holding me gently as I heal. Amen.

Affirmation

I open my heart to God with honesty. In His presence, my pain is met with comfort and healing.

Your Reflection Space

Day 15

I Will Not Pretend Anymore

There comes a moment in healing when you realize that pretending no longer serves you. For a long time, you may have smiled through pain, remained silent through disappointment, and carried on with strength even when your heart felt heavy. Pretending can feel like protection. It can feel easier to appear strong than to admit that you are hurting. Yet over time, this quiet performance can leave you feeling disconnected from your true self.

Choosing not to pretend anymore is an act of courage. It means allowing yourself to be honest about what you feel and what you need. It means releasing the pressure to appear unshaken when your heart has been through difficult experiences. This honesty is not a sign of weakness. It is a step toward authenticity and healing. When you stop pretending, you create space for truth, compassion, and restoration to enter your life.

God welcomes your honesty. Psalm 32:3–5 (NIV) "When I kept silent, my bones wasted away through my groaning all day long... Then I acknowledged my sin to you and did not cover up my iniquity... And you forgave the guilt of my sin."

He does not expect you to hide your struggles or present a perfect image. He sees beyond appearances and understands the depth of your experiences. When you come before Him with sincerity, you are met with acceptance and care. You can speak openly about what you feel without fear of judgment.

In His presence, there is freedom to be real and to receive the comfort you need. Releasing the need to pretend also allows you to care for yourself more gently. You begin to recognize your emotional needs and honor them with kindness. You permit yourself to rest, to feel, and to heal without rushing. This shift brings a sense of relief and authenticity that supports true renewal. You no longer have to carry the burden of appearing strong at all times.

Today is an invitation to embrace honesty with yourself and with God. You do not have to hide your emotions or suppress your experiences. You can show up as you are and trust that you are still worthy of love and healing. As you release the need to pretend, you move closer to a life that feels genuine, peaceful, and whole.

Healing Reflection

In what ways have you been pretending to be stronger or less affected than you truly feel, and how might honesty bring relief?

Reset Prayer

Compassionate Father,

You know my heart completely and understand what I have been carrying. Today I release the need to pretend that everything is fine. Help me to be honest with myself and with You. Give me the courage to acknowledge my feelings and the grace to heal gently. Surround me with Your peace and remind me that I am safe to be real in Your presence. Thank You for receiving me with love and understanding. Amen.

Affirmation

I release the need to pretend. I honor my truth and allow healing to begin within me.

Your Reflection Space

THE RESET

Healing. Boundaries. Spiritual Realignment

Day 16

Today I Choose Healing

Healing often begins with a quiet decision. It is not always a dramatic moment or a sudden change. Sometimes it starts with a gentle choice made within the heart. A choice to move forward. A choice to release what has been heavy. A choice to believe that restoration is possible. Today can be that moment for you. A moment where you choose healing, even if it unfolds one small step at a time. Choosing healing does not mean that everything is suddenly resolved. It does not erase the past or remove every difficult emotion. Instead, it opens the door to a new way of living. It allows you to move from simply enduring life to intentionally caring for your heart and spirit. When you choose healing, you begin to treat yourself with compassion rather than criticism. You begin to believe that peace and renewal are possible for your life. Jeremiah 30:17 (NIV) — "But I will restore you to health and heal your wounds,' declares the Lord."

God honors your decision to heal. He meets you with grace and supports every step you take toward wholeness. You do not have to figure everything out on your own. With each small act of self-care, each honest prayer, and each moment of reflection, you are moving closer to a restored sense of peace. Healing may not always be quick, but it is always meaningful. Every step forward matters.

Today is an opportunity to set a gentle intention for your journey. You can choose to let go of what has weighed on you and to open your heart to restoration.

You can choose to treat yourself with kindness and patience. You can choose to believe that even after difficult seasons, your life can still hold joy, purpose, and calm.

Let this be a day where you affirm your desire for healing. Not because everything is perfect, but because you are worthy of peace and renewal. Each time you choose healing, you create space for hope to grow. Each time you move forward with intention, you strengthen the foundation for a life that feels balanced and whole.

Healing Reflection

What does choosing healing look like for you today, and what is one gentle step you can take toward your well-being?

Reset Prayer

Loving Father,

Today I make a quiet decision to choose healing. I release what has weighed heavily on my heart and open myself to Your restoring presence. Guide me as I take small steps toward peace and renewal. Give me patience with myself and the courage to move forward with hope. Help me to trust that You are working within me even when I cannot see immediate change. Thank You for walking beside me and strengthening me as I heal. Amen.

Affirmation

Today I choose healing. With patience and faith, I am moving toward peace and wholeness.

Your Reflection Space

Day 17

Resetting My Mind

The mind holds many thoughts throughout the day. Some bring peace and clarity, while others create worry and heaviness. Over time, repeated thoughts can shape how you see yourself, your circumstances, and your future. When your mind has been filled with stress, disappointment, or self-doubt, it can feel difficult to experience calm and hope. Resetting your mind is a gentle process of creating space for thoughts that support healing and peace.

You may have become accustomed to thinking in ways that reflect past pain or present uncertainty. When difficult experiences linger in your memory, they can influence how you interpret new situations. You may expect disappointment or anticipate challenges before they arise. These thought patterns are understandable, especially if you have been through emotionally taxing seasons. Yet your mind can be renewed with patience and intention.

God offers peace that begins within the mind and extends into the heart. When you bring your thoughts before Him, you allow space for clarity and calm to replace confusion and worry. Resetting your mind does not mean ignoring reality or pretending everything is perfect. It means choosing to focus on what nurtures your well-being rather than what drains your spirit. It means gently guiding your thoughts toward truth, hope, and possibility. As you begin to reset your mind, speak to yourself with kindness. Replace harsh self-criticism with understanding.

Replace fearful assumptions with trust in God's presence. Each time you choose a peaceful thought over a fearful one, you create a new pattern that supports healing. Over time, these small shifts bring a sense of stability and emotional balance. Today is an invitation to become aware of your thoughts without judgment. Notice what fills your mind and gently guide it toward peace. You do not have to control every thought perfectly. Start with clear intentions and a sense of patience. As you invite God into your thought life, He will help you cultivate a mindset that supports healing and renewal.

Healing Reflection

What thoughts have been weighing on your mind lately, and which of them are ready to be released or replaced with more peaceful ones?

Reset Prayer

Heavenly Father,

You know the thoughts that fill my mind and the worries that sometimes overwhelm me. Today I ask for a renewal of my mind. Help me to release thoughts that bring fear, doubt, or heaviness. Replace them with peace, clarity, and hope. Guide my thinking so that it reflects truth and supports my healing. Thank You for bringing calm to my mind and steadiness to my heart as I move forward. Amen.

Affirmation

My mind is being renewed with peace and clarity. I choose thoughts that support my healing and growth.

Your Reflection Space

Day 18

Releasing What I Cannot Control

Many things in life rest beyond your control. The decisions made by others can often leave you feeling powerless or uncertain. When you care deeply, it is natural to want to fix, manage, or guide everything toward a desired outcome. Yet carrying the weight of what you cannot control can become exhausting and overwhelming.

You may have spent time and energy trying to hold everything together. You may have tried to anticipate problems, protect others, or prevent disappointment. Over time, this constant effort can create tension within your mind and body. It can feel as though you must remain vigilant at all times. This kind of strain quietly drains your peace and leaves little room for rest.

Releasing what you cannot control is not about giving up. It is about recognizing the limits of your responsibility and trusting God with what lies beyond your reach. You don't have to shoulder the entire burden of every situation. Some things require surrender rather than effort. When you release the need to control everything, you allow yourself to breathe more freely and rest more deeply. Proverbs 3:5–6 (NIV) "Trust in the Lord with all your heart and lean not on your own understanding. In all your ways submit to Him, and He will make your paths straight."

God sees the concerns that fill your thoughts and the situations that feel uncertain. He understands your desire for stability and resolution. When you place these matters in His hands, you are not abandoning them.

You are entrusting them to a wisdom and care greater than your own. This act of surrender can bring a sense of calm that effort alone cannot provide. Today is an opportunity to gently loosen your grip on what you cannot change. Notice what feels heavy and ask yourself whether it truly belongs in your hands. Some things are meant to be carried by God, not by you. As you release control, you create space for peace to settle into your heart and mind. In that space, you may begin to feel lighter and more grounded.

Allow yourself to rest in the understanding that you are supported. You do not have to manage every detail of life on your own. By trusting God with what you cannot control, you move forward with greater ease and renewed strength.

Healing Reflection

What situation or concern have you been trying to control that may be ready to be released into God's care?

Reset Prayer

Faithful Father,

You see the things I have been trying to control and the worries that have weighed on my heart. Today, I release them into Your hands. Help me to trust that You are working even when I cannot see the outcome. Give me peace where I feel anxious and rest where I feel overwhelmed. Teach me to surrender what I cannot change and to walk forward with confidence in Your care. Thank You for holding my life with wisdom and love. Amen.

Affirmation

I release what I cannot control and trust that God is guiding my life with care and wisdom.

Your Reflection Space

Day 19

Giving Myself Permission to Rest

There are times when the body continues moving, but the heart and mind long for stillness. You may have become so accustomed to meeting responsibilities and caring for others that rest feels unfamiliar or even undeserved. Yet rest is not a luxury reserved for certain moments. It is a necessary part of healing and renewal. Without it, your spirit becomes weary, and your strength begins to fade.

You may have learned to push through exhaustion and continue despite feeling overwhelmed. Perhaps you believed that resting meant falling behind or letting others down. Over time, this mindset can create a pattern of constant effort without enough restoration. The heart and mind need moments of quiet and care to remain balanced and healthy. When you permit yourself to rest, you are not neglecting your responsibilities. You are nurturing your well-being so you can move forward with greater clarity and strength. Exodus 33:14 (NIV) — "My Presence will go with you, and I will give you rest."

God invites you into a rhythm that includes both effort and rest. He understands your need for renewal and does not expect you to carry on endlessly without pause. When you allow yourself to rest, you acknowledge that your strength is not limitless and that you are worthy of care and restoration. Rest can be physical, emotional, and spiritual. It may be a moment of stillness, a quiet prayer, or a gentle release of pressure.

Today is an invitation to treat yourself with kindness. Notice where you feel tired and consider what kind of rest would bring comfort to your heart.

It may be a few quiet moments alone, a slower pace, or simply allowing yourself to breathe without rushing. Each small act of rest contributes to healing and balance. You do not have to earn rest by exhaustion. You deserve it simply because you are human and worthy of care.

Allow this day to include moments of gentleness. Release the pressure to do everything perfectly or immediately. When you rest, your strength is renewed, and your perspective becomes clearer. With God's presence surrounding you, rest becomes a sacred space where healing continues to unfold.

Healing Reflection

Where in your life do you feel most in need of rest, and what small step can you take today to honor that need?

Reset Prayer

Loving Father,

You see the weariness within me and the places where I feel tired. Today, I permit myself to rest in Your presence. Help me to release the pressure to keep going without pause. Restore my strength and bring calm to my heart and mind. Teach me to value rest as a part of healing and renewal. Thank You for holding me gently and renewing me with Your peace. Amen.

Affirmation

I permit myself to rest. In stillness and trust, my strength is being renewed.

Your Reflection Space

Day 20

God Is Still Writing My Story

There are moments when life feels uncertain, and you begin to wonder how your story will unfold. When you look back on what you have experienced, you may see chapters filled with unexpected turns, disappointments, or changes you did not anticipate. It can be easy to assume that what has already happened will determine what comes next. Yet your story is not finished. Each day brings the possibility of new beginnings and gentle restoration.

God is not limited by what has already taken place in your life. He sees beyond the present moment and understands the full journey ahead. Even when certain chapters feel difficult to read, He continues to write with care and purpose. What may seem like an ending can become the beginning of something meaningful and steady. You may not see the full picture yet, but your life is still unfolding in ways that hold potential and hope.

It is natural to question what lies ahead, especially when the past has been challenging. You may wonder whether things can truly change or whether peace and joy will return. In those moments, remember that your story is still being shaped. Every step you take toward healing, every moment of honesty, and every prayer you offer becomes part of the journey forward. Nothing you have experienced is beyond God's ability to restore and transform.

Today is an invitation to view your life with renewed perspective. Rather than focusing only on what has been lost or altered, consider what is still possible. God continues to guide your steps with patience and wisdom.

He can bring beauty from what once felt broken and clarity from what once felt confusing. Your story is not defined by one chapter. It is shaped by the ongoing presence of grace and growth.

Allow yourself to move forward with quiet trust. You do not need to know every detail of what lies ahead. You can take one step at a time, knowing that your life remains in caring hands. With each new day, a new line is written in your story. With each moment of faith, your path becomes clearer and more peaceful.

Healing Reflection

When you think about your life as an unfolding story, what hopes or possibilities do you want to believe are still ahead for you?

Reset Prayer

Faithful Father,

Thank You for continuing to guide my life even when I feel uncertain about the future. Help me to trust that my story is still being written with care and purpose. Where I feel discouraged, bring renewed hope. Where I feel unsure, bring clarity. Teach me to move forward with faith, knowing that You are leading me toward peace and growth. Thank You for walking beside me and shaping my journey with wisdom and love. Amen.

Affirmation

My story is not finished. With faith and hope, I move forward into the life still unfolding before me.

Your Reflection Space

Day 21

Breaking Soul Ties with the Past

There are connections and experiences from the past that can remain with us long after they have ended. Memories, emotional attachments, and unresolved feelings sometimes linger quietly in the heart. These ties can influence how you see yourself and how you move through your present life. You may find yourself revisiting old conversations, old pain, or old expectations that no longer serve your well-being. Letting go of these attachments can feel challenging, especially when they were once meaningful.

Breaking emotional ties with the past does not mean denying what you experienced or pretending it did not matter. It means recognizing that you are no longer required to carry everything forward. Some connections were part of a previous season and have fulfilled their place in your journey. Holding on too tightly can prevent you from experiencing the peace and clarity that are available to you now. Release allows you to move forward with a lighter heart. Isaiah 43:18–19 (NIV) declares — "Forget the former things; do not dwell on the past. See, I am doing a new thing! Now it springs up; do you not perceive it? I am making a way

God understands the depth of every attachment you have formed and the emotions connected to them. He does not rush you to let go without care. Instead, He gently invites you to release what no longer brings life or peace. When you place these attachments in His hands, you create space for healing and renewal. You allow your heart to rest from the weight of what has already passed and to open to what is present.

Today is an opportunity to acknowledge any lingering emotional ties that may still affect you.

Notice what feels heavy or unresolved. Rather than holding on tightly, consider offering those feelings to God with trust. Release is not about forgetting. It is about freeing your heart so that it can live fully in the present. As you loosen your hold on what once was, you create room for new strength and deeper peace.

Allow this day to mark a gentle shift. You are not bound to every experience from your past. You are allowed to move forward with clarity and freedom. With God's guidance, you can release what no longer serves you and embrace a future that feels lighter and more hopeful.

Healing Reflection

What emotional ties or memories from the past feel ready to be released so that you can move forward with greater peace?

Reset Prayer

Loving Father,

You know the connections and memories that still weigh on my heart. Today, I bring them before You with trust. Help me to release what no longer serves my well-being. Free my heart from attachments that keep me bound to the past. Fill the space within me with Your peace and clarity. Guide me as I move forward with freedom and renewed strength. Thank You for walking with me as I heal and grow. Amen.

Affirmation

I release what belongs to the past. My heart is free to move forward with peace and clarity.

Your Reflection Space

Day 22

Forgiving Without Reopening Wounds

Forgiveness can feel like one of the most difficult steps in healing. When you have been hurt or disappointed, it is natural to protect your heart. You may fear that forgiving someone means allowing the same pain to happen again or dismissing what you experienced. Yet forgiveness is not about forgetting what happened or pretending that it did not matter. It is about freeing your heart from the weight of resentment and choosing peace for yourself.

You can forgive without reopening wounds. Forgiveness does not require you to return to harmful situations or lower your boundaries. It simply means releasing the emotional hold that pain may have on you. When you hold on to anger or resentment, it can quietly affect your peace and well-being. Letting go does not excuse what occurred. It allows you to move forward without the burden of carrying it. Ephesians 4:31–32 (NIV) —"Get rid of all bitterness, rage and anger. Be kind and compassionate to one another, forgiving each other, just as in Christ God forgave you."

God understands how deeply certain experiences may have affected you. He does not pressure you to forgive before you are ready. Instead, He gently guides you toward a place where forgiveness becomes a gift you give yourself. When you bring your pain before Him, He begins to soften the places that feel hardened. Over time, what once felt impossible can become manageable as His peace fills your heart.

Forgiveness is a process that unfolds with patience. You may not feel ready all at once, and that is perfectly acceptable.

Each time you choose to release a small piece of resentment, you create space for healing. Each time you choose peace over bitterness, you strengthen your emotional and spiritual well-being. You remain in control of your boundaries while allowing your heart to rest from the weight of past hurt.

Today is an invitation to consider what forgiveness might look like for you. It may be a quiet decision within your heart rather than a spoken conversation. It may be a simple willingness to release anger little by little. As you take this step, trust that God is guiding you with compassion. Forgiveness does not diminish your strength. It reflects the courage of a heart that chooses peace and freedom.

Healing Reflection

Is there someone or something you may be ready to forgive to free your heart, even if that forgiveness happens quietly within you?

Reset Prayer

Merciful Father,

You know the pain I have experienced and the emotions that remain. Today, I ask for Your help in learning to forgive in a way that protects my peace and honors my healing. Soften my heart where it feels hardened and bring calm where there is tension. Help me release resentment without reopening wounds. Guide me with wisdom as I move toward freedom and peace. Thank You for walking with me through this process with patience and love. Amen.

Affirmation

I choose forgiveness as a path to peace. My heart is free to heal and move forward with strength.

Your Reflection Space

Day 23

Boundaries Are Not Bitterness

There may have been times when you felt that protecting your peace meant disappointing others. You may have worried that setting limits would make you seem unkind or distant. Many caring and compassionate women struggle with this tension. They want to love others well, yet they also need space to protect their emotional and spiritual well-being. Learning to set boundaries can feel unfamiliar, especially if you are used to putting others first.

Boundaries are not acts of bitterness. They are acts of wisdom and self-respect. A boundary defines what feels safe and healthy for your heart and mind. It allows you to engage with others from a place of clarity rather than exhaustion. When you set gentle and firm limits, you are not rejecting people. You are honoring your need for balance and peace. This allows your relationships to grow within a healthier, more respectful, and emotionally balanced space.

God values your well-being and does not expect you to live without protection or rest. He understands the importance of caring for your heart as you move through life. Setting boundaries can be a way of stewarding the life and peace He has entrusted to you. It allows you to give from a place of wholeness rather than depletion. When your heart is protected, your kindness and compassion can flow more naturally and sustainably. Proverbs 4:23 (NIV) — "Above all else, guard your heart, for everything you do flows from it."

At first, setting boundaries may feel uncomfortable. You may worry about how others will respond or whether you are doing the right thing.

With time and practice, you will begin to see that healthy limits create stability rather than division. They help you remain grounded and emotionally balanced. They remind you that your needs are worthy of attention and care.

Today is an opportunity to reflect on where boundaries may be needed in your life. Consider what brings you peace and what drains your energy. Ask yourself what small step you can take to honor your well-being. Boundaries do not have to be harsh or confrontational. They can be gentle, clear, and rooted in self-respect. As you practice setting them, you move toward a life that feels more balanced and peaceful.

Healing Reflection

Where in your life do you feel a need for healthier boundaries, and what gentle step can you take to protect your peace?

Reset Prayer

Wise and Loving Father,
You know my heart and the areas where I feel stretched or overwhelmed. Help me to set healthy boundaries that honor my well-being and reflect Your wisdom. Give me the courage to protect my peace without guilt or fear. Teach me that caring for myself allows me to care for others in a healthier way. Guide my words and actions so they are rooted in kindness and clarity. Thank You for helping me live with balance and strength. Amen.

Affirmation

Setting boundaries is an act of wisdom and self-respect. I honor my peace with clarity and grace.

Your Reflection Space

Day 24

I Am Allowed to Choose Me

There are times in life when you may have prioritized the needs of others over your own, often at the cost of your own well-being. You may have given your time, energy, and care freely, often without pausing to consider what you needed in return. While generosity and compassion are beautiful qualities, continually neglecting your own well-being can leave you feeling depleted and unseen. Choosing yourself does not mean you care less about others. It means you are acknowledging that your needs are important as well.

You are allowed to choose what supports your peace, your healing, and your growth. This choice is not selfish. It is an act of self-respect and awareness. When you choose yourself, you are acknowledging that your emotional and spiritual health deserves attention. You are permitting yourself to rest when you are tired, to step back when you feel overwhelmed, and to pursue what brings you calm and clarity. Mark 12:31 (NIV) —"Love your neighbor as yourself."

God values you deeply and cares about every aspect of your life, including your well-being. He does not ask you to neglect yourself to serve others. Instead, He invites you to live with balance and wisdom. When you care for your heart and mind, you are better able to live with purpose and compassion. Choosing yourself can become an act of stewardship over the life God has entrusted to you.

At times, choosing yourself may feel unfamiliar or uncomfortable. You may worry about how others will respond or whether you are doing the right thing. Over time, you will begin to see that honoring your needs brings stability and peace.

It allows you to live with greater authenticity and confidence. You can give to others from a place of wholeness rather than exhaustion.

Today is an invitation to honor your own well-being with kindness.

Notice what you need emotionally and spiritually. Consider one small way you can choose yourself today, whether it is rest, reflection, or setting a gentle boundary. Each time you choose what supports your healing, you strengthen your sense of balance and self-worth. You are worthy of the same care and attention you so freely give to others.

Healing Reflection

In what area of your life do you need to begin choosing your well-being with greater intention and compassion?

Reset Prayer

Loving Father,

Thank You for caring about every part of my life and well-being. Help me to recognize that my needs matter and that I am allowed to choose what supports my peace and healing. Give me wisdom to care for myself with balance and courage to make choices that honor my heart. Guide me as I learn to live with greater clarity and self-respect. Thank You for walking beside me as I grow stronger and more grounded each day. Amen.

Affirmation

I am allowed to choose what nurtures my peace and healing. My well-being matters and deserves care.

Your Reflection Space

Day 25

Rebuilding My Self-Worth

There may have been moments in your life when your sense of worth felt shaken. Words, experiences, or disappointments can sometimes cause you to question your value. You may have questioned your worthiness and whether you deserved the care and respect you desired. Over time, these doubts can quietly affect how you see yourself and how you move through the world. Rebuilding self-worth begins with recognizing that your value has never been lost, even in difficult seasons.

Your worth is not determined by how others have treated you or by what you have experienced. Mistakes, setbacks, and the opinions of others do not define your worth. Your value exists within you and has always been present. Sometimes it becomes hidden beneath pain or discouragement, but it never disappears. When you begin to see yourself through a lens of compassion and truth, your sense of worth can slowly be restored. Psalm 139:14 (NIV) — "I praise you because I am fearfully and wonderfully made; your works are wonderful; I know that full well."

God sees you with love and understanding. He does not measure your value by your past or by the expectations of others. He sees your heart, your intentions, and the strength it has taken for you to continue moving forward. When you allow His perspective to shape how you see yourself, you begin to understand that you are worthy of kindness, respect, and peace. This understanding becomes the foundation for rebuilding your self-worth.

Rebuilding self-worth is a gentle process. It begins with small acts of self-kindness and honest reflection. Speak to yourself with patience rather than criticism.

Notice the qualities within you that reflect resilience and compassion. Each time you choose to treat yourself with respect, you strengthen your sense of value. Over time, these choices create a more stable and confident understanding of who you are.

Today is an invitation to see yourself with fresh eyes. Acknowledge your strength, your growth, and your capacity for healing. You are not defined by what has happened to you. You are defined by the depth of your spirit and the potential that still lies ahead. As you rebuild yourself worth, you create space for peace, confidence, and renewed purpose to grow within you.

Healing Reflection

What experiences or messages have affected your sense of self-worth, and what truth about yourself are you ready to believe instead?

Reset Prayer

Loving Father,
 You know every experience that has shaped how I see myself. Today, I ask for Your help in rebuilding my sense of worth. Remind me that my value is not determined by past pain or the opinions of others. Help me to see myself through Your eyes of compassion and truth. Strengthen my confidence and guide me as I learn to treat myself with kindness and respect. Thank You for restoring my heart and reminding me of the worth You placed within me. Amen.

Affirmation

My worth is steady and unchanging. I honor myself with kindness, respect, and truth.

Your Reflection Space

Day 26

Healing My Inner Woman

Within you lives a part of yourself that has carried every experience, every memory, and every emotion throughout your life. This inner woman holds your joys as well as your wounds. She remembers the times you felt safe and cherished, and she also remembers the moments when you felt overlooked or hurt. Sometimes she becomes quiet and guarded, protecting herself from further pain. Healing begins when you gently turn toward her with compassion and care.

You may not always have given yourself the nurturing you needed. Life can move quickly, and responsibilities can take priority over personal reflection. Yet the inner woman within you still longs to feel seen, valued, and supported. She desires kindness and reassurance. When you begin to acknowledge her needs, you create a pathway for healing that reaches deep within your heart.

God sees every part of who you are, including the tender places that may feel fragile. He understands the experiences that shaped your inner world and the emotions that remain. His presence offers comfort and restoration for the parts of you that need gentle care. When you invite Him into your healing, He helps you nurture yourself with patience and understanding.

You begin to treat your heart with the same compassion He extends to you. Healing your inner woman is not about revisiting every painful moment. It is about offering yourself the kindness and reassurance that may have been missing. Speak to yourself with gentleness.

Allow yourself moments of quiet reflection and care. Notice when you need rest, encouragement, or comfort, and respond with patience rather than criticism. These small acts of nurturing create a sense of safety within you.

Today is an opportunity to connect with the deeper part of yourself that longs for healing and peace. Consider what your inner woman needs most in this moment. It may be reassurance, forgiveness, or simple acknowledgment. Offer that to yourself with love and grace. As you care for the woman within, you strengthen your sense of wholeness and open the door for continued renewal.

Healing Reflection

What does your inner self need most right now to feel comforted, supported, and valued?

Reset Prayer

Compassionate Father,
You know every part of my heart and every experience that has shaped me. Today, I ask for Your guidance as I care for the inner parts of myself that need healing. Help me to treat myself with gentleness and understanding. Bring comfort where I feel tender and peace where I feel unsettled. Teach me to nurture my heart with patience and grace as You continue to restore me. Thank You for walking with me through this journey of healing and renewal. Amen.

Affirmation

I nurture the woman within me with kindness and compassion. I am worthy of gentle healing and care.

Your Reflection Space

Day 27

Speaking Kindly to Myself Again

The way you speak to yourself shapes how you feel about who you are and how you move through each day. Your inner voice has the power to comfort or to criticize, to encourage or to discourage. Over time, harsh self-talk can quietly become a habit, especially if you have experienced disappointment or self-doubt. You may have learned to hold yourself to impossible standards or to focus on what you feel you lack rather than what you have overcome.

Speaking kindly to yourself again is an important part of healing. It is not about ignoring mistakes or pretending everything is perfect. It is about choosing words that support growth and compassion instead of judgment. When you speak to yourself with patience and understanding, you create an environment within your heart where healing can flourish. Your mind begins to feel calmer, and your spirit becomes lighter. I

God speaks to you with love and truth. His voice is not harsh or condemning. It is steady, patient, and full of grace. When you align your inner voice with this same gentleness, you begin to see yourself through a lens of compassion. You start to recognize that you are still growing and learning. Each day becomes an opportunity to treat yourself with the same kindness you would offer someone you care about deeply. Isaiah 43:4 (NIV) "You are precious and honored in my sight... and I love you."

At first, changing your inner dialogue may feel unfamiliar. You may catch yourself falling back into old patterns of self-criticism. When this happens, pause and gently redirect your thoughts. Replace harsh words with affirming ones. Remind yourself that growth takes time and that you are worthy of encouragement. With practice, your inner voice will become more supportive and nurturing.

Today is an invitation to listen to how you speak to yourself. Notice your thoughts without judgment. Where you hear criticism, offer kindness instead. Where you feel discouraged, speak words of reassurance. Each kind word you offer yourself strengthens your sense of peace and self-respect. Over time, this gentle practice creates a more compassionate and supportive relationship with yourself.

Healing Reflection

What kind of words have you been speaking to yourself lately, and how can you begin to replace them with more compassionate and encouraging ones?

Reset Prayer

Loving Father,
You know the thoughts I carry and the words I sometimes speak to myself. Help me to replace harshness with kindness and criticism with understanding. Teach me to see myself through Your eyes of grace and truth. Guide my thoughts so they bring encouragement and peace. Thank You for helping me build a more compassionate and loving relationship with myself each day. Amen.

Affirmation

I speak to myself with kindness and compassion. My words support my healing and growth.

Your Reflection Space

Day 28

Letting Go of Shame

Shame can settle quietly within the heart and influence how you see yourself. It may come from past mistakes, painful experiences, or words that were spoken to you during vulnerable moments. Shame often tells you that you are not enough or that you should hide parts of yourself. Over time, it can create a sense of heaviness that affects your confidence and peace. Yet shame does not define who you are, and it does not have the final say over your life.

You are more than the experiences that have caused you pain or regret. Every person carries moments they wish had unfolded differently. These moments do not erase your worth or diminish your value. They are simply part of your journey as a human being, learning and growing through life. When you hold on to shame, you carry a burden that was never meant to define you. Releasing it allows your heart to breathe and your spirit to feel lighter.

God sees you with compassion and understanding. He does not view you through the lens of shame or condemnation. He sees your heart, your intentions, and your desire to grow. When you bring your feelings of shame before Him, you are met with mercy and grace. His love gently reminds you that you are worthy of healing and renewal. You do not have to hide or withdraw. You can stand in the truth that you are valued and deeply cared for. Letting go of shame is a gradual process. It begins with acknowledging what you have been carrying and choosing not to let it define your identity.

Each time you speak to yourself with compassion instead of judgment, you weaken the hold that shame once had. Each time you remember that your worth remains intact, you strengthen your sense of freedom. Healing grows in these moments of self-acceptance and grace. Today is an invitation to release any shame you have been holding. You do not need to carry it into the next chapter of your life. You are allowed to move forward with dignity and peace. As you let go of shame, you create space for confidence, clarity, and renewed hope to take root within you.

Healing Reflection

What feelings of shame or self-judgment have you been carrying, and what truth about your worth are you ready to embrace instead?

Reset Prayer

Merciful Father,

You know the feelings of shame that sometimes weigh on my heart. Today, I bring them before You with honesty and trust. Help me to release what does not belong to my identity. Remind me that I am worthy of love, healing, and grace. Replace shame with peace and self-acceptance. Guide me as I move forward with renewed confidence in who I am. Thank You for seeing me with compassion and restoring my heart. Amen.

Affirmation

I release shame and embrace grace. My worth remains steady, and I move forward with confidence and peace.

Your Reflection Space

Day 29

Trusting God While Healing

Healing often unfolds in ways that cannot always be seen or measured right away. There may be days when you feel strong and hopeful, and other days when emotions rise unexpectedly. This gentle and sometimes uneven process can feel uncertain. In those moments, trusting God becomes a quiet anchor. Trust does not require you to have every answer. It simply asks that you believe you are being guided and cared for as you heal.

You may wonder at times whether your healing is truly happening. When progress feels slow, it can be easy to doubt or grow discouraged. Yet healing often takes place beneath the surface before it becomes visible. Small shifts in your thoughts, your responses, and your sense of peace are signs that something meaningful is taking place within you. Each moment you choose to move forward with faith strengthens your path.

God understands the vulnerability that comes with healing. He sees the effort it takes to face emotions honestly and to release what has been heavy. He does not rush your journey or expect perfection. Instead, He walks beside you with patience and compassion. Even when you cannot feel immediate change, His presence remains steady. Trusting Him allows you to rest in the knowledge that your healing is unfolding with purpose. Trust does not eliminate every moment of uncertainty. It provides a sense of steadiness within it. When you choose to trust, you shift your focus from what feels uncertain to the One who is constant. You remind yourself that you are not walking this path alone. Each step you take, no matter how small, is supported by a presence that does not waver.

Today is an invitation to place your healing journey gently in God's hands. You do not need to monitor every detail or question every step. Simply continue forward with faith and openness. As you trust God with your process, you allow peace to grow within you. Over time, that peace becomes a steady foundation for the life you are rebuilding. Isaiah 41:10 (NIV) "So do not fear, for I am with you; do not be dismayed, for I am your God. I will strengthen you and help you; I will uphold you with my righteous right hand."

Healing Reflection

In what ways can you deepen your trust in God as you continue your healing journey, even when progress feels slow or uncertain?

Reset Prayer

Faithful Father,

You know my heart and the journey I am walking. Help me to trust You as I continue to heal. When I feel uncertain, remind me that You are guiding my steps. When I feel discouraged, I renew my hope and strength. Teach me to rest in Your presence and believe that healing is unfolding even when I cannot see it clearly. Thank You for walking beside me with patience and love. Amen.

Affirmation

I trust God with my healing journey. With faith and patience, I am being gently restored each day.

Your Reflection Space

Day 30

My Peace Is Non-Negotiable

There comes a moment in healing when you begin to recognize the value of your peace. After walking through emotional strain, disappointment, or uncertainty, you start to understand how essential calm and stability are for your well-being. Peace is not simply the absence of conflict. It is a sense of steadiness within your heart and mind that allows you to move through life with clarity and balance. Protecting that peace becomes an important part of caring for yourself.

You may have spent time in environments or relationships that disrupted your sense of calm. You may have tried to maintain harmony by sacrificing your own comfort. Over time, this can leave you feeling unsettled and drained. Choosing peace now means recognizing what supports your emotional and spiritual health and what disturbs it. It means becoming aware of what brings calm and what creates tension within you.

God desires for you to live with a sense of peace that grounds and strengthens you. His presence offers a steady place where your heart can rest and be renewed. When you begin to value your peace as something sacred, you naturally make choices that support it. You learn to step back from what creates unnecessary stress and to move toward what nurtures calm and clarity. This is not about avoiding responsibility. It is about living with wisdom and intention. John 14:27 (NIV) "Peace I leave with you; my peace I give you. I do not give to you as the world gives. Do not let your hearts be troubled and do not be afraid."

Declaring that your peace is non-negotiable does not mean you will never face challenges. It means you choose not to allow unnecessary stress or emotional strain to take root in your life. You permit yourself to step away from situations that disturb your well-being. You prioritize moments of stillness and reflection. Each time you honor your peace, you strengthen your sense of stability and self-respect.

Today is an opportunity to affirm the importance of your inner calm. Consider what supports your peace and what disrupts it. Make a gentle commitment to protect what brings you steadiness and clarity. As you do, you create an environment within yourself where healing can continue to grow. Your peace is valuable. It deserves to be protected and nurtured with care.

Healing Reflection

What habits, situations, or boundaries will help you protect and maintain your peace moving forward?

Reset Prayer

Loving Father,

Thank You for the gift of peace that sustains my heart and mind. Help me to recognize what supports my well-being and what disrupts it. Give me wisdom to make choices that protect my peace and courage to step away from what brings unnecessary stress. Fill my heart with calm and clarity as I move forward. Thank You for guiding me into a life that feels balanced and grounded in Your presence. Amen.

Affirmation

My peace is valuable and worth protecting. I choose calm, clarity, and balance each day.

Your Reflection Space

Day 31

Walking Away from What Drains Me

There are times in life when you begin to notice what quietly drains your energy. Certain situations, conversations, or environments may leave you feeling exhausted rather than renewed. You may feel tension in your spirit after interactions that once felt manageable. Over time, these experiences can weigh heavily on your emotional and spiritual well-being. Recognizing what drains you is not a sign of weakness. It is a sign of growing awareness and wisdom.

You may have stayed in certain situations longer than your heart could comfortably hold. Out of loyalty, kindness, or responsibility, you may have continued giving even when you felt depleted. While your intentions may have been sincere, constant emotional strain can affect your sense of balance and peace. Walking away from what drains you does not mean you are unkind or uncaring. It means you are choosing to care for yourself with honesty and clarity.

God desires for you to live with a sense of peace and steadiness. He understands when your energy has been stretched too thin. When you begin to step back from what consistently drains you, you create room for restoration and calm. This process does not always require dramatic changes. Sometimes it begins with small, thoughtful decisions that protect your well-being. Each step toward balance strengthens your ability to live with greater clarity and purpose.2 Timothy 1:7 (NIV) "For the Spirit God gave us does not make us timid, but gives us power, love, and self-discipline." Walking away from what drains you can feel unfamiliar at first.

You may wonder whether you are doing the right thing or worry about how others will respond. Over time, you will begin to notice the difference in how you feel. As you release what exhausts you, you create space for what nourishes and strengthens your spirit. Your energy becomes more focused, and your heart feels lighter.

Today is an invitation to notice what brings fatigue to your heart and mind. Consider whether some patterns or situations consistently leave you feeling depleted. Ask yourself what gentle adjustments you can make to protect your energy and peace. Each small choice you make in support of your well-being is a step toward a life that feels more balanced and calmer. You deserve to live in a way that sustains and restores you.

Healing Reflection

What situations, habits, or interactions leave you feeling emotionally drained, and what steps can you take to create healthier distance or balance?

Reset Prayer

Wise and Loving Father,
You see the areas of my life that feel heavy and draining. Help me recognize what no longer supports my well-being. Give me the courage to step back from what exhausts my spirit and wisdom to move toward what brings peace. Guide my choices so they reflect balance and clarity. Thank You for helping me create a life that feels steady, peaceful, and aligned with Your care. Amen.

Affirmation

I release what drains my energy and move toward what restores my peace and strength.

Your Reflection Space

Day 32

Choosing Emotional Safety

Emotional safety is a quiet but powerful need within every heart. It is the sense of being able to exist without constant tension, fear, or uncertainty. When you feel emotionally safe, you can think clearly, rest peacefully, and move through life with greater confidence. When that safety is missing, your mind and spirit can feel unsettled. Choosing emotional safety is an important step in protecting your well-being and continuing your healing journey.

You may not always have recognized how important emotional safety is. At times, you may have remained in environments or relationships that caused stress or confusion because you hoped things would improve. You may have adjusted yourself to maintain peace, even when it came at a personal cost. Over time, this can create a sense of imbalance and emotional fatigue. Choosing emotional safety now means honoring what allows your heart to feel calm and secure.

God cares deeply about your sense of peace and stability. He does not desire for you to live in constant emotional strain. His presence offers a steady foundation where you can feel supported and grounded. As you grow in awareness, you can begin to recognize what nurtures your sense of safety and what disrupts it. With this understanding, you can make gentle choices that support your healing and peace. Psalm 4:8 (NIV) "In peace I will lie down and sleep, for you alone, Lord, make me dwell in safety." Choosing emotional safety may involve setting boundaries, limiting exposure to stressful situations, or creating moments of quiet reflection.

It may also involve surrounding yourself with people who treat you with kindness and respect. These choices are not acts of withdrawal from life. They are acts of wisdom and self-care. Each step you take toward emotional safety strengthens your sense of stability and clarity.

Today is an invitation to reflect on what emotional safety means for you. Notice when you feel calm and supported, and notice when you feel tense or unsettled. Consider one small step you can take to create a greater sense of safety within your daily life. As you honor this need, you move closer to a life that feels balanced and peaceful. You deserve to live in an environment that supports your healing and well-being.

Healing Reflection

What situations or environments make you feel emotionally safe, and what changes might help you experience more of that safety in your daily life?

Reset Prayer

Loving Father,

You know my heart and the places where I feel safe or unsettled. Guide me as I seek emotional safety and peace. Help me recognize what supports my well-being and give me the courage to move away from what disturbs it. Surround me with Your calming presence and lead me toward environments and relationships that nurture my spirit. Thank You for caring about my peace and guiding me with wisdom each day. Amen.

Affirmation

I choose emotional safety and peace. I honor what nurtures my well-being and protects my heart.

Your Reflection Space

Day 33

Resetting My Faith

There are moments in life when your faith may feel quieter than it once did. After walking through disappointment, uncertainty, or emotional strain, it is natural to question and reflect. You may find yourself wondering where God was during certain seasons or why some prayers seemed unanswered. These thoughts do not mean your faith is lost. They simply reflect a heart that is seeking understanding and reassurance.

Resetting your faith does not require starting over completely. It is a gentle return to trust and connection. Faith can be renewed in quiet and meaningful ways. It may begin with a simple prayer, a moment of reflection, or an honest conversation with God. You do not need perfect words or complete clarity. You only need a willing heart and a desire to draw closer once again.

God welcomes you exactly where you are. He is not distant or disappointed by your questions. He understands every emotion you carry and every moment of doubt you have experienced. His presence remains steady even when your faith feels fragile. When you come to Him honestly, you are met with compassion and patience. He gently restores what feels worn and strengthens what feels uncertain. Lamentations 3:22–23 (NIV) "Because of the Lord's great love, we are not consumed, for his compassions never fail. They are new every morning; great is your faithfulness."

Resetting your faith may involve letting go of expectations that no longer serve you. It may mean releasing the idea that faith must always feel strong or unwavering.

Real faith often grows through honest reflection and renewed trust. As you allow yourself to reconnect with God sincerely and openly, you begin to feel a sense of peace returning. Your faith becomes less about perfection and more about relationship.

Today is an invitation to return to God with honesty and openness. You do not need to hide your questions or pretend that everything feels clear. Simply bring your heart as it is. Allow this moment to be a fresh beginning for your faith. As you reconnect, you will find that God's presence remains steady and welcoming. Your faith can be renewed gently and naturally, one step at a time.

Healing Reflection

In what ways would you like to reconnect with God and renew your faith in this season of your life?

Reset Prayer

Faithful Father,
You know my heart and the questions that sometimes arise within me. Today, I come to You with honesty and openness. Renew my faith and strengthen my trust in Your presence. Help me release doubts that weigh on my spirit and fill me with peace and reassurance. Guide me as I reconnect with You in a deeper and more meaningful way. Thank You for welcoming me with patience and love as I continue this journey. Amen.

Affirmation

My faith is being renewed with peace and trust. I walk forward knowing God is near and guiding me.

Your Reflection Space

Day 34

When God Feels Silent

There are moments in life when God may seem quiet or distant. You may pray and wait for clarity, comfort, or direction, yet feel as though no answer comes. During these times, it can be easy to wonder whether your prayers are being heard or whether you are walking alone. This experience can feel unsettling, especially when you long for reassurance and guidance.

When God feels silent, it does not mean He is absent. Silence is not the same as distance. Often, God is present in ways that are gentle and unseen. He may be working quietly within your circumstances or strengthening you in ways that will become clear later. While it may not always feel this way, His care remains constant and steady. Your prayers are never ignored, and your journey is never unnoticed. Psalm 66:19–20 (NIV) "But God has surely listened and has heard my prayer. Praise be to God, who has not rejected my prayer or withheld his love from me!"

Silence can also be a space where growth and reflection take place. In quiet moments, you may begin to notice subtle forms of guidance and comfort. A sense of calm may emerge where there was once anxiety. A new perspective may form where confusion once lingered. These gentle shifts are signs that something meaningful is happening beneath the surface. Even when you cannot hear immediate answers, you can trust that your life is still being guided with care.

God understands how difficult it can be to wait without clear direction. He sees your longing for reassurance and your desire to feel close to Him. You do not need to hide these feelings.

You can bring your questions and uncertainty into prayer with honesty. In doing so, you create space for comfort and peace to settle within your heart. Trust does not require constant certainty. It grows quietly through patience and openness.

Today is an invitation to remain open even in the quiet. Allow yourself to sit with God without expecting immediate answers. Let this moment be one of gentle trust rather than frustration. Even when you cannot feel or hear what you hope for, God remains present. His care continues to surround you, guiding your steps in ways that will unfold with time.

Healing Reflection

How do you usually respond when you feel that God is quiet, and what might help you remain open and trusting during those moments?

Reset Prayer

Loving Father,

There are times when I feel uncertain and long to hear Your guidance more clearly. Help me to trust that You are present even in quiet moments. Calm my heart when I feel restless and remind me that I am never alone. Give me patience to wait and peace to trust Your timing. Thank You for walking beside me and holding my life with wisdom and care. Amen.

Affirmation

Even in quiet moments, God is present with me. I trust that I am being guided with care and love.

Your Reflection Space

Day 34

When God Feels Silent

There are moments in life when God may seem quiet or distant. You may pray and wait for clarity, comfort, or direction, yet feel as though no answer comes. During these times, it can be easy to wonder whether your prayers are being heard or whether you are walking alone. This experience can feel unsettling, especially when you long for reassurance and guidance.

When God feels silent, it does not mean He is absent. Silence is not the same as distance. Often, God is present in ways that are gentle and unseen. He may be working quietly within your circumstances or strengthening you in ways that will become clear later. While it may not always feel this way, His care remains constant and steady. Your prayers are never ignored, and your journey is never unnoticed. Lamentations 3:25–26 (NIV) "The Lord is good to those whose hope is in him, to the one who seeks him; it is good to wait quietly for the salvation of the Lord."

Silence can also be a space where growth and reflection take place. In quiet moments, you may begin to notice subtle forms of guidance and comfort. A sense of calm may emerge where there was once anxiety. A new perspective may form where confusion once lingered. These gentle shifts are signs that something meaningful is happening beneath the surface. Even when you cannot hear immediate answers, you can trust that your life is still being guided with care.

God understands how difficult it can be to wait without clear direction. He sees your longing for reassurance and your desire to feel close to Him.

You do not need to hide these feelings. You can bring your questions and uncertainty into prayer with honesty. In doing so, you create space for comfort and peace to settle within your heart. Trust does not require constant certainty. It grows quietly through patience and openness.

Today is an invitation to remain open even in the quiet. Allow yourself to sit with God without expecting immediate answers. Let this moment be one of gentle trust rather than frustration. Even when you cannot feel or hear what you hope for, God remains present. His care continues to surround you, guiding your steps in ways that will unfold with time.

Healing Reflection

How do you usually respond when you feel that God is quiet, and what might help you remain open and trusting during those moments?

Reset Prayer

Loving Father,
There are times when I feel uncertain and long to hear Your guidance more clearly. Help me to trust that You are present even in quiet moments. Calm my heart when I feel restless and remind me that I am never alone. Give me patience to wait and peace to trust Your timing. Thank You for walking beside me and holding my life with wisdom and care. Amen.

Affirmation

Even in quiet moments, God is present with me. I trust that I am being guided with care and love.

Your Reflection Space

Day 35

Learning to Be Still

Life can move quickly, filling your days with responsibilities, decisions, and constant motion. In the midst of this pace, stillness can feel unfamiliar or even uncomfortable. You may feel as though you must keep moving, thinking, or planning to maintain control. Yet there is quiet strength in learning to be still. Stillness creates space for reflection, clarity, and renewal. It allows your heart and mind to settle and find peace.

Being still does not mean doing nothing. It means allowing yourself to pause without pressure. It is a moment where you step away from constant activity and give your spirit room to breathe. In stillness, you become more aware of your thoughts and emotions. You begin to notice what you need and what you are ready to release. This gentle awareness supports healing and helps you move forward with greater clarity.

God often speaks in quiet ways that are easier to notice when your mind is calm. When you slow down and allow yourself to be still, you create an opportunity to feel His presence more deeply. Stillness becomes a space where reassurance and peace can gently enter your heart. Psalm 46:10 (NIV) says, "Be still and know that I am God." It is not about achieving perfection in your thoughts or emotions. It is simply about being present and open.

Learning to be still may take practice, especially if you are used to staying busy. You may notice restlessness at first. With patience, you will begin to experience the comfort that comes from quiet moments.

Even a few minutes of stillness can bring a sense of calm and balance. Over time, these moments become a source of strength and clarity. Today is an invitation to create a small space for stillness. It may be a few quiet moments in the morning or a pause during the day. Allow yourself to sit without rushing or planning. Breathe slowly and let your thoughts settle. In this stillness, you may begin to feel a gentle sense of peace. You may notice a clearer perspective or a renewed sense of strength. Stillness allows your heart to rest and your spirit to be refreshed.

Healing Reflection

What might help you create moments of stillness in your daily life so that your heart and mind can rest and reset?

Reset Prayer

Gentle Father,

Help me learn to be still in Your presence. Calm my thoughts and quiet the restlessness within me. Teach me to pause without fear and to trust that I am safe in moments of stillness. Renew my heart and mind as I rest in Your care. Thank You for the peace that comes when I slow down and allow Your presence to surround me. Amen.

Affirmation

In stillness, I find peace. My heart and mind are renewed as I rest gently in God's presence.

Your Reflection Space

Day 36

Releasing Bitterness Completely

Bitterness can quietly take root when pain remains unaddressed for too long. It often begins as hurt or disappointment that has not yet found a place of healing. Over time, these feelings can harden and create a sense of heaviness within the heart. You may notice lingering resentment or a guarded outlook that makes it difficult to feel at peace. While these responses are understandable, bitterness can slowly drain your emotional and spiritual energy.

Releasing bitterness does not mean denying what you have experienced. It does not require you to forget or excuse what caused you pain. It means choosing not to let those experiences control your present peace. Holding on to bitterness keeps your heart connected to past wounds. Letting it go allows you to move forward with greater freedom and clarity. Ephesians 4:31-32 "Get rid of all bitterness, rage and anger, brawling and slander, along with every form of malice. Be kind and compassionate to one another, forgiving each other, just as in Christ God forgave you." This process is not always immediate, but it becomes possible with patience and intention.

God understands every hurt you have carried. He sees the moments that left you feeling disappointed or misunderstood. When you bring these feelings before Him, He meets you with compassion rather than judgment. His presence offers a place where bitterness can soften and eventually release its hold. You are not asked to handle this alone. You are gently guided toward peace as you allow His grace to work within you.

Releasing bitterness completely is a gradual journey. It begins with acknowledging what you feel and then choosing to let peace replace resentment. Each time you release a negative thought or memory that fuels bitterness, you take a step toward healing. Over time, your heart becomes lighter and more open to calm and understanding. You begin to experience freedom from the emotional weight that bitterness creates.

Today is an invitation to examine what you may still be holding within your heart. Notice any lingering resentment or tension. Bring these feelings into prayer with honesty and trust. Allow yourself to imagine what it would feel like to be free from this weight. As you choose release, even in small ways, you move toward a life that feels more peaceful and balanced.

Healing Reflection

Is there any lingering bitterness in your heart that you are ready to release so you can experience greater peace and freedom?

Reset Prayer

Merciful Father,
You see the hurt I have carried and the moments that left me feeling wounded. Today I choose to release bitterness from my heart. Help me let go of resentment and replace it with peace. Heal the places within me that still feel tender and guide me toward freedom and calm. Thank You for helping me move forward without the weight of past pain. Amen.

Affirmation

I release bitterness and welcome peace. My heart is free to heal and move forward with calm and clarity.

Your Reflection Space

Day 37

Breaking the Cycle of Pain

There are patterns in life that can quietly repeat themselves if they are not gently examined and released. Sometimes pain from the past influences how you respond in the present. You may notice familiar feelings returning in new situations or old fears shaping current decisions. These patterns do not mean you are failing. They simply reflect experiences that have not yet fully healed. Recognizing them is the first step toward change.

Breaking the cycle of pain begins with awareness. When you notice a familiar emotional response or repeated pattern, pause and reflect without judgment. Ask yourself what this moment is teaching you about your needs and your healing. You are not meant to remain trapped in cycles that cause distress. You can grow, learn, and respond in new ways that support your peace and well-being. As Scripture reminds us, "If anyone is in Christ, the new creation has come: The old has gone, the new is here!" — 2 Corinthians 5:17 (NIV)

God sees every pattern that has shaped your life. He understands the experiences that influenced your reactions and the moments that left lasting impressions. When you bring these patterns before Him, you invite guidance and clarity into your journey. His presence helps you see yourself with compassion rather than criticism. With His support, you can begin to respond differently and create new pathways rooted in peace. Breaking the cycle of pain does not happen all at once. It unfolds through small, intentional choices. Each time you respond with calm instead of fear, with understanding instead of self-blame, you create a new direction.

These choices may feel subtle at first, yet they hold great power. Over time, they reshape your experience and help you move forward with greater confidence and balance.

Today is an invitation to notice any patterns that no longer serve your well-being. Approach them with kindness rather than judgment. Consider what new response or perspective might bring healing and peace. With God's guidance, you can step out of old cycles and into a new way of living. You are not bound by what has been. You are free to move toward what brings growth and renewal.

Healing Reflection

What pattern or emotional cycle in your life are you ready to break so that you can move forward with greater peace and clarity?

Reset Prayer

Loving Father,
You see the patterns that have shaped my experiences and the cycles I am ready to release. Help me recognize what no longer serves my well-being. Give me wisdom to respond in healthier ways and courage to step into new patterns of peace and growth. Guide my thoughts and actions so they reflect healing and renewal. Thank You for leading me into a life that feels freer and more balanced. Amen.

Affirmation

I am breaking old cycles with wisdom and grace. Each step I take leads me toward peace and renewal.

Your Reflection Space

Day 38

I Am Not Who Hurt Me

There are moments when the pain caused by others can begin to shape how you see yourself. Words spoken in anger, actions rooted in misunderstanding, or experiences of rejection can leave deep impressions. Over time, it is possible to internalize what happened and begin to believe that those experiences define who you are. Yet the truth remains that what was done to you does not determine your identity. You are not the hurt you experienced. You are not the disappointment someone caused. You are not the rejection you endured. Those moments were part of your story, but they are not the essence of who you are. Your identity is rooted in your character, your resilience, and the depth of your spirit. Scripture reminds us, "But you are a chosen people... God's special possession." — 1 Peter 2:9 (NIV) When you separate yourself from the pain others caused, you begin to reclaim a sense of clarity and strength.

God sees you beyond every wound and every difficult experience. He does not define you by what others have done or by the moments that left you feeling diminished. He sees your heart with compassion and truth. When you begin to view yourself through this lens, you can release the weight of false definitions. You are free to see yourself as worthy, capable, and deeply valued.

Reclaiming your identity may take time and gentle reflection. You may need to remind yourself often that you are not defined by past pain. Each time you affirm your true worth, you weaken the hold that those experiences once had on your sense of self. Over time, a stronger and more confident understanding of who you are begins to emerge. This clarity brings peace and stability.

Today is an invitation to release any identity shaped by past hurt. Notice where you may have allowed painful experiences to influence how you see yourself. Replace those thoughts with truth and compassion. You are not the one who hurt you. You are a person of strength, dignity, and value. As you embrace this truth, you create space for a renewed sense of confidence and peace within your life.

Healing Reflection

In what ways have past experiences shaped how you see yourself, and what truth about your identity are you ready to embrace instead?

Reset Prayer

Loving Father,

You know the experiences that have influenced how I see myself. Today, I ask for Your help in releasing any false beliefs rooted in past hurt. Remind me that I am not defined by what others have done to me. Help me see myself through Your eyes of truth and compassion. Strengthen my confidence and restore my sense of identity. Thank You for reminding me that I am worthy, valued, and whole. Amen.

Affirmation

I am not defined by past hurt. I embrace my true identity with strength, dignity, and peace.

Your Reflection Space

Day 39

Strength I Didn't Know I Had

There are moments in life when you look back and realize that you have endured more than you ever thought you could. Situations that once felt overwhelming did not break you. Seasons that seemed unbearable did not defeat you. Even when you felt fragile, you continued moving forward. Within you is a quiet strength that has carried you through every difficult moment. As Scripture reminds us, "I can do all this through him who gives me strength." — Philippians 4:13 (NIV) Sometimes you only recognize that strength when you pause and reflect on how far you have come.

You may not always feel strong. There are days when exhaustion or uncertainty can make you question your resilience. Yet strength is not always loud or visible. Often it appears as quiet endurance, gentle perseverance, and the decision to keep going even when the path feels unclear. Each time you faced a challenge and continued forward, you demonstrated a strength that deserves recognition and honor.

God has been present in every moment of your journey. He has seen your courage, even when you did not recognize it yourself. He has sustained you in ways that may not always have been visible but were always present. The strength you carry is not yours alone. It is strengthened by the support and guidance that surrounds you each day. When you acknowledge this strength, you begin to see yourself with greater confidence and appreciation.

Recognizing your strength does not mean ignoring your need for rest or support. It simply means honoring the resilience that exists within you. You have faced moments that required courage and patience. You have navigated uncertainty and continued to grow. Each experience has contributed to the person you are becoming. The strength you carry today is the result of every step you have taken, even when those steps felt small.

Today is an invitation to acknowledge the strength you possess. Reflect on what you have overcome and how you have continued moving forward. Allow yourself to feel a sense of appreciation for your resilience. You are stronger than you once believed, and that strength continues to grow. As you recognize it, you create a deeper sense of confidence and peace within yourself.

Healing Reflection

What challenges have you faced that reveal the strength and resilience you carry within you today?

Reset Prayer

Faithful Father,

Thank You for sustaining me through every challenge and every uncertain moment. Help me to recognize the strength You have placed within me. Remind me that I am capable, resilient, and supported by Your presence. When I feel weak, I renew my confidence and restore my courage. Guide me as I continue moving forward with faith and quiet strength. Thank You for walking with me and strengthening me each day. Amen.

Affirmation

I honor the strength within me. I am resilient, supported, and growing stronger each day.

Your Reflection Space

Day 40

My Healing Is Happening

Healing does not always arrive in dramatic or visible ways. Often it unfolds quietly and gently, one small step at a time. You may not always notice the progress you are making because you are living within the process each day. Yet if you pause and reflect, you may begin to see subtle changes. You may notice that certain thoughts feel lighter or that moments of peace come more easily. These are signs that healing is taking place within you.

There may still be moments when you feel tender or uncertain. Healing does not mean that every difficult emotion disappears at once. It means that you are moving forward with greater awareness and strength. Each time you choose calm over fear, kindness over self-criticism, and trust over worry, you are participating in your own restoration. These small choices accumulate and gradually reshape how you experience life.

God is present in every step of your healing journey. He sees what is changing within you, even when those changes feel subtle. He understands your desire for peace and your effort to move forward with faith. When you feel discouraged or wonder whether progress is being made, remember that healing often happens beneath the surface before it becomes fully visible. Trust that something meaningful is unfolding within you. Recognizing that your healing is happening allows you to move forward with patience and hope. You do not need to rush or measure your progress against any timeline. Your journey is unique and unfolding in its own way.

Each day you continue to show up for yourself with honesty and care, you strengthen the foundation for lasting peace. Every step you take matters, even when it feels small.

Today is an invitation to acknowledge the healing that is already taking place within you. Notice the ways you have grown and the moments where you feel stronger or more at peace. Celebrate these shifts with gratitude. You are moving forward, even if the progress feels gradual. Trust that your heart is being restored and that each day brings you closer to a life that feels balanced and whole.

Healing Reflection

What changes, no matter how small, have you noticed within yourself that show healing is already taking place?

Reset Prayer

Loving Father,
Thank You for the healing that is quietly unfolding within me. Even when I cannot see every change, help me trust that You are working in my life. Give me patience with my journey and peace in each step forward. Strengthen my heart and remind me that progress is happening. Thank You for guiding me toward wholeness and renewal each day. Amen.

Affirmation

Healing is happening within me. With patience and faith, I am becoming stronger, calmer, and more whole each day.

Your Reflection Space

PART THREE

BECOMING

Confidence. Identity. New Life

Day 41

I Am Becoming Whole Again

There is a quiet restoration that takes place when you begin to heal from what once felt overwhelming. Little by little, the scattered pieces of your heart begin to come together. What once felt broken starts to feel mended. Scripture reminds us, "He heals the brokenhearted and binds up their wounds." — Psalm 147:3 (NIV). What once felt uncertain begins to feel steady. Becoming whole again does not happen in a single moment. It unfolds gradually as you allow yourself to grow, reflect, and receive peace.

You may remember a time when you felt more certain of who you were and where you were going. Difficult experiences may have shaken that sense of clarity, leaving you feeling disconnected or unsure. Yet wholeness is not something that disappears forever. It is something that can be rebuilt with patience and care. Every step you take toward healing helps restore a sense of balance and completeness within you.

God sees the work taking place in your heart. He understands the effort it takes to move beyond pain and toward renewal. Even when you feel uncertain, He continues guiding you gently forward. His presence brings a steady reassurance that you are not alone in this process. As you allow His peace to settle within you, the pieces of your life begin to align in new and meaningful ways.

Becoming whole again does not mean returning to who you were before every challenge. It means growing into a deeper and more resilient version of yourself. You carry the wisdom gained through your experiences and the strength developed through your healing. This new sense of wholeness reflects both your journey and your growth.

It is steady, grounded, and filled with quiet confidence. Today is an invitation to recognize the restoration taking place within you. Notice the ways you feel more centered and aware. Acknowledge the progress you have made, even if it feels gradual. You are not the same person you were when this journey began. You are becoming whole again, with greater strength and clarity. Allow yourself to move forward with hope and trust in the process unfolding within you.

Healing Reflection

In what ways do you feel yourself becoming stronger, more balanced, or more whole than you felt before?

Reset Prayer

Gracious Father,

Thank You for the healing and restoration taking place within me. Help me to recognize the ways I am becoming whole again. Strengthen my heart and guide me as I continue to grow. Remind me that every step forward brings me closer to peace and balance. Thank You for walking beside me and restoring my spirit with patience and love. Amen.

Affirmation

I am becoming whole again. With each step forward, I grow stronger, steadier, and more at peace.

Your Reflection Space

Day 42

Becoming a Woman of Peace

Peace is not something you wait to find someday. It is something you begin to cultivate within yourself. After walking through seasons of stress, disappointment, and emotional strain, there comes a moment when you realize that peace is no longer optional. It becomes essential. Becoming a woman of peace means choosing calm over chaos and clarity over confusion. It means protecting the steadiness you have worked so hard to restore.

You may have spent years navigating environments that felt unsettled or unpredictable. You may have carried worries that kept your mind restless and your heart tense. Over time, this can make peace feel unfamiliar. Yet peace is your natural state when you allow yourself to release what disturbs your spirit. It grows when you begin to make choices that support balance and emotional safety.

God desires for you to live with a sense of peace that strengthens and steadies you. His presence offers a calm foundation that remains steady even when life feels uncertain. As you draw closer to Him, you begin to notice that peace is not dependent on perfect circumstances. It grows from within and becomes a guiding force in how you think, speak, and respond. As Scripture reminds us, "Let the peace of Christ rule in your hearts..." — Colossians 3:15 (NIV). You become less reactive and more grounded. You move with intention rather than pressure. Becoming a woman of peace involves gentle awareness. Notice what disrupts your calm and what nurtures it.

Choose environments, conversations, and habits that support your well-being. Speak to yourself with kindness and allow moments of stillness to restore you. Each peaceful choice strengthens your sense of stability and confidence. Over time, peace becomes a natural part of who you are rather than something you must constantly search for.

Today is an invitation to embrace peace as a way of life. You are not striving for perfection. You are allowing calm and clarity to guide your steps. As you continue your healing journey, peace will become more familiar and more present. You are becoming a woman who moves through life with steadiness, wisdom, and grace. That peace will not only bless your own life but will also gently influence those around you.

Healing Reflection

What does becoming a woman of peace look like in your daily life, and what choices will help you nurture that peace within yourself?

Reset Prayer

Loving Father,
Thank You for the peace You offer that steadies my heart and mind. Help me become a woman who chooses peace in my thoughts, my words, and my actions. Guide me away from what disturbs my spirit and lead me toward what nurtures calm and clarity. Fill my heart with Your presence so that peace becomes a natural part of who I am. Thank You for shaping me into a woman who walks with grace, strength, and quiet confidence. Amen.

Affirmation

I am becoming a woman of peace. Calm, clarity, and steadiness guide my heart and my life.

Your Reflection Space

Day 43

Becoming Emotionally Free

Emotional freedom begins when you realize that your peace no longer has to depend on what others do or say. For a long time, your emotions may have been shaped by circumstances beyond your control. You may have felt pulled by the expectations of others, weighed down by past experiences, or affected by words and actions that left you feeling uncertain. Becoming emotionally free means gently releasing the hold these things have had on your inner world.

Emotional freedom does not mean you stop caring. It means you stop carrying what was never meant to be yours. You learn to respond rather than react. You learn to protect your peace without closing your heart. This freedom allows you to feel without becoming overwhelmed and to love without losing yourself. It is a balanced place where your emotions are acknowledged but no longer control your sense of stability.

God desires for you to live with this kind of freedom. He understands every emotional weight you have carried and every moment you felt bound by circumstances or memories. When you place your heart in His care, you begin to experience a sense of release. You realize that you are not defined by what once hurt you. As Scripture reminds us, "So if the Son sets you free, you will be free indeed." — John 8:36 (NIV). You are not required to relive what has already passed. With His guidance, you can move forward with clarity and strength.

Becoming emotionally free is a process of gentle release. It may involve letting go of old narratives about yourself or releasing the need for validation from others.

It may involve forgiving, setting boundaries, or choosing peace in situations that once caused distress. Each time you choose calm over emotional entanglement, you take a step toward freedom. Over time, this freedom becomes a steady part of your life.

Today is an invitation to embrace emotional freedom with intention. Notice where you feel tied to past pain or present pressure. Consider what it would feel like to release that hold and breathe more freely. You deserve to live with a sense of lightness and calm. As you continue your journey, emotional freedom will allow you to experience life with greater clarity and peace.

Healing Reflection

What emotional weight or attachment are you ready to release so that you can experience greater freedom and peace within yourself?

Reset Prayer

Gracious Father,

You know the emotions I have carried and the places where I have felt bound or overwhelmed. Today I ask for emotional freedom. Help me release what no longer serves my peace and guide me toward balance and clarity. Teach me to respond with wisdom and to protect the calm within my heart. Thank You for leading me into a life where I can feel free, steady, and at peace. Amen.

Affirmation

I am becoming emotionally free. My heart is light, steady, and grounded in peace.

Your Reflection Space

Day 44

I Am Not Broken Anymore

There may have been a time when you felt as though something inside you had shattered. Painful experiences, deep disappointments, or seasons of loss can create the feeling that you have been broken beyond repair. When life brings unexpected wounds, it can be easy to question your strength and your ability to feel whole again. Yet healing has a quiet way of restoring what once felt damaged. You are not broken beyond healing. You are being restored with care and intention. Joel 2:25–26 (NIV) "I will restore to you the years that the locusts have eaten. You will have plenty to eat until you are full, and you will praise the name of the Lord your God, who has worked wonders for you."

What you experienced may have hurt deeply, but it did not destroy your essence. Beneath every wound, your spirit has remained present and resilient. Even in moments when you felt fragile, something within you continued to endure. That quiet strength has carried you through each difficult season and brought you to this point of awareness and renewal. You are not defined by what has hurt you. You are defined by the strength that continues to rise within you.

God does not see you as broken. He sees you as whole and worthy, even in the midst of healing. He understands every part of your journey and the moments that left you feeling diminished. His presence has been with you through each step, gently guiding you toward restoration. When you allow yourself to see through His eyes of compassion, you begin to understand that nothing within you is beyond healing. You are being renewed in ways both visible and unseen.

Releasing the belief that you are broken is a powerful step toward freedom. It allows you to view yourself with kindness and respect rather than judgment. You begin to recognize that you are growing, learning, and becoming stronger. Each moment of healing adds to your sense of wholeness. Each step forward confirms that you are not defined by past pain but by the strength and grace that continue to shape your life.

Today is an invitation to embrace the truth of your restoration. You are not broken anymore. You are healing, growing, and becoming more whole with each passing day. Allow yourself to stand in this truth with confidence and peace. Your journey has not diminished you. It has strengthened and refined you. You are worthy of a life that feels balanced, peaceful, and complete.

Healing Reflection

What beliefs or memories made you feel broken, and what truth can you now embrace about your strength and wholeness?

Reset Prayer

Loving Father,
Thank You for restoring my heart and reminding me that I am not broken. Help me release any belief that I am beyond healing or repair. Fill me with the truth of my worth and the strength You have placed within me. Guide me as I continue to grow into wholeness and peace. Thank You for walking beside me and restoring every part of my life with compassion and care. Amen.

Affirmation

I am not broken anymore. I am whole, restored, and moving forward with strength and peace.

Your Reflection Space

Confidence Is Returning

There was a time when your confidence may have felt steady and natural. You moved through life with a sense of assurance and clarity about who you were. Then life happened. Disappointments, challenges, and unexpected changes may have shaken that confidence and left you questioning yourself. You may have doubted your decisions or hesitated where you once felt certain. Yet confidence is not permanently lost. It can return gently and steadily as you continue to heal. Scripture reminds us, "Do not throw away your confidence; it will be richly rewarded." — Hebrews 10:35 (NIV)

Confidence does not always reappear dramatically. Often it returns quietly through small moments of courage and self-trust. Each time you make a choice that honors your well-being, you strengthen your sense of confidence. Each time you speak kindly to yourself and acknowledge your growth, you rebuild trust within your heart. These small acts become the foundation for a stronger and more grounded sense of self.

God has always seen the strength within you, even when you questioned it. He understands the experiences that caused you to feel uncertain or hesitant. Yet He also knows the resilience that remains within your spirit. As you continue moving forward, His presence gently restores your sense of confidence. You begin to see yourself not through the lens of past pain but through the truth of who you are becoming. Allow confidence to return at its own pace. You do not need to force it or measure it against who you once were. The confidence that is emerging now is deeper and more grounded.

It is rooted in wisdom gained through experience and in a clearer understanding of your worth. This renewed confidence supports your decisions, your voice, and your ability to move forward with clarity.

Today is an invitation to notice where confidence is quietly returning within you. Acknowledge the moments when you feel more certain or at ease. Celebrate the progress you have made, even if it feels gradual. Confidence is growing within you once again. With each step you take, you are becoming more secure, more aware, and more at peace with who you are.

Healing Reflection

Where have you noticed your confidence beginning to return, and how can you continue to nurture it with patience and trust?

Reset Prayer

Gracious Father,

Thank You for restoring my confidence and strengthening my spirit. Help me trust the growth taking place within me. When I feel uncertain, remind me of the strength and wisdom You have placed inside me. Guide my steps and give me courage to move forward with clarity and peace. Thank You for renewing my confidence and helping me walk with assurance once again. Amen.

Affirmation

My confidence is returning. I trust myself, honor my growth, and move forward with calm and strength.

Your Reflection Space

Day 46

Reintroducing Myself to Joy

There may have been a time when joy felt natural and easy. You smiled without effort, laughed freely, and found pleasure in simple moments. Then life brought experiences that felt heavy or overwhelming. Over time, joy may have seemed distant or unfamiliar. When the heart carries pain for a long season, it can forget how to welcome joy without hesitation. Yet joy has not disappeared from your life. It has simply been waiting for space to return.

Reintroducing yourself to joy is a gentle and intentional process. It does not require grand moments or dramatic changes. Joy often begins quietly through small experiences that bring warmth and lightness. A peaceful morning, a kind conversation, or a moment of stillness can become the beginning of joy's return. As you allow yourself to notice these moments, your heart begins to open again.

You are allowed to experience joy without guilt or hesitation. Choosing joy does not diminish what you have endured. It honors the healing that is taking place within you. Joy and healing can exist together. In fact, joy often becomes a sign that your heart is restoring itself. Scripture reminds us, in Psalm 30:11 (NIV), "You turned my wailing into dancing and clothed me with joy." Each moment of happiness, no matter how small, reminds you that life still holds beauty and meaning.

God delights in your joy and desires for you to experience peace and lightness once again. His presence offers reassurance that joy is not something you must earn.

It is something you can receive with gratitude. As you continue your journey, allow yourself to notice what brings a gentle smile to your heart. These moments are invitations to reconnect with a sense of happiness that is both genuine and renewing.

Today is an opportunity to welcome joy back into your life. Pay attention to what lifts your spirit, even slightly. Allow yourself to enjoy it fully without overthinking. Joy may feel unfamiliar at first, but it will become more natural with time. You are not leaving your healing behind. You are allowing joy to become part of your healing. As you reintroduce yourself to joy, you create space for a life that feels lighter, calmer, and more fulfilling.

Healing Reflection

What simple moments or experiences bring you a sense of joy, and how can you make space for more of them in your life?

Reset Prayer

Loving Father,
Thank You for the gift of joy that gently returns to my life. Help me welcome moments of happiness without fear or hesitation. Teach me to notice the beauty and peace around me each day. Restore my heart and fill it with lightness and gratitude. Thank You for reminding me that joy is a part of my healing and a reflection of Your goodness. Amen.

Affirmation

I welcome joy back into my life. My heart is open to peace, lightness, and renewed happiness.

YOUR REFLECTION SPACE

Day 47

Softness Without Weakness

There may have been times when you felt that being soft meant being vulnerable in ways that could lead to hurt. You may have believed that strength required a hardened exterior or constant emotional guard. Life experiences can sometimes create the impression that gentleness must be sacrificed to remain protected. Yet true strength and softness can exist together. Softness does not mean weakness. It reflects a heart that has chosen healing over hardness.

Softness is the ability to remain compassionate without losing yourself. It allows you to respond with calm rather than defensiveness and to move through life with grace rather than tension. A soft heart does not mean you accept mistreatment or ignore your needs. It means you approach life with wisdom and clarity while maintaining kindness toward yourself and others. This balance creates a quiet confidence that supports both strength and peace. The good book says, in 2 Corinthians 12:9 (NIV) But he said to me, 'My grace is sufficient for you, for my power is made perfect in weakness." Therefore, I will boast all the more gladly about my weaknesses, so that Christ's power may rest on me.

God created you with the capacity for both strength and gentleness. He does not ask you to become hardened to protect yourself. Instead, He offers guidance that helps you maintain a tender heart while also setting healthy boundaries. When you trust His presence, you can remain open and compassionate without feeling vulnerable or unprotected. Your softness becomes a reflection of healing rather than a sign of fragility.

Learning to live with softness without weakness may take time and practice. You may need to remind yourself that kindness toward yourself and others is a form of strength. Each time you choose calm over harshness or understanding over defensiveness, you strengthen your sense of balance. You demonstrate that true strength is not found in emotional distance but in the ability to remain grounded and peaceful.

Today is an invitation to embrace both your strength and your softness. Allow yourself to move through life with grace and confidence. You can protect your peace while remaining gentle in spirit. You can set boundaries while still being compassionate. Softness and strength can exist together within you, creating a sense of stability and calm that supports your continued healing and growth.

Healing Reflection

How can you embrace gentleness and compassion within yourself while still maintaining healthy strength and boundaries?

Reset Prayer

Gracious Father,
Thank You for creating me with both strength and gentleness. Help me embrace a soft heart without feeling weak or unprotected. Teach me to move through life with wisdom, kindness, and confidence. Guide me as I set healthy boundaries while maintaining compassion. Thank You for helping me live with balance, peace, and quiet strength each day. Amen.

Affirmation

My softness is strength. I move through life with grace, wisdom, and a peaceful heart.

Your Reflection Space

Day 48

Stronger Than My Past

There are moments when memories of the past may try to remind you of who you once were or what you once endured. Certain experiences may have left deep impressions, and at times, it can feel as though those moments still hold power over your present. Yet the truth is that you are no longer standing in those same places. You have grown, learned, and continued forward. As Scripture reminds us, "In all these things we are more than conquerors through him who loved us." — Romans 8:37 (NIV) You are stronger than anything that tried to define you before.

Your past is part of your story, but it does not control your future. Every challenge you faced required courage, even when you did not feel strong. Every difficult season shaped your resilience and deepened your understanding of yourself. The strength you carry today is not accidental. It has been formed through perseverance and the quiet determination to keep moving forward.

God has walked with you through every chapter of your life. He has seen the moments when you felt uncertain and the times when you questioned your own strength. Even then, He continued guiding you toward growth and renewal. His presence has been a steady source of support, helping you move beyond what once felt overwhelming. With His guidance, you are no longer bound by what has already happened. You are free to move forward with clarity and confidence. Recognizing that you are stronger than your past allows you to live with greater freedom. You can acknowledge what you have experienced without allowing it to define your identity.

You can honor your journey while embracing who you are becoming. Each step you take now reflects the wisdom and resilience gained through every challenge you have overcome.

Today is an invitation to stand in the truth of your strength. Reflect on how far you have come and how much you have grown. You are not the same person you were in moments of pain or uncertainty. You are stronger, wiser, and more aware. Allow yourself to move forward with confidence, knowing that your past has shaped your resilience but does not limit your future.

Healing Reflection

What experiences from your past have revealed your strength, and how can you continue moving forward with confidence and self-trust?

Reset Prayer

Faithful Father,

Thank You for carrying me through every season of my life. Help me recognize the strength You have built within me. Remind me that my past does not define my future. Give me confidence to move forward with courage and clarity. Strengthen my heart and guide my steps as I continue growing and healing. Thank You for walking with me and helping me become stronger each day. Amen.

Affirmation

I am stronger than my past. I move forward with confidence, wisdom, and renewed strength.

Your Reflection Space

Day 49

I Deserve Stability

There is a deep sense of calm that comes from stability. It allows your mind to rest and your heart to feel secure. After seasons of uncertainty or emotional strain, the desire for stability becomes even more meaningful. You may long for consistency, peace, and a sense of grounding that allows you to breathe without tension. Wanting stability is not asking for too much. It is a natural and healthy desire for a life that feels balanced and steady.

You deserve stability in your environment, your relationships, and your inner world. Stability does not mean that life will always be perfect or without challenges. It means that you are building a foundation that supports your well-being. It means choosing what brings consistency and peace rather than chaos or confusion. Each time you move toward what feels steady and reliable, you strengthen your sense of security.

God cares deeply about your need for stability. He understands the importance of feeling safe and supported as you move through life. His presence offers a steady foundation that does not shift with circumstances. As Scripture reminds us, "He will be the sure foundation for your times..." — Isaiah 33:6 (NIV). As you lean into His guidance, you begin to create a life that reflects calm and balance. You become more intentional about what you allow into your space and more aware of what nurtures your peace. Building stability often begins with small, consistent choices. Establishing routines that support your well-being, surrounding yourself with trustworthy influences, and honoring your need for rest all contribute to a more grounded life.

These choices may seem simple, yet they create a sense of order and reassurance that allows your heart to settle. Over time, stability becomes a natural part of your daily experience.

Today is an invitation to affirm your worthiness of a stable and peaceful life. Notice where stability already exists and where it can be strengthened. Allow yourself to choose what supports your sense of calm and reliability. You are not meant to live in constant uncertainty. You deserve a life that feels secure, balanced, and steady. As you continue forward, stability will become a strong and comforting presence within your journey.

Healing Reflection

What areas of your life feel stable and supportive, and where can you begin creating more consistency and balance?

Reset Prayer

Loving Father,
Thank You for being a steady presence in my life. Help me build stability in my thoughts, my choices, and my environment. Guide me toward what supports peace and consistency. Give me wisdom to choose what nurtures my well-being and courage to release what disrupts it. Thank You for helping me create a life that feels grounded, calm, and secure. Amen.

Affirmation

I deserve stability and peace. My life is becoming more balanced, steady, and secure each day.

Your Reflection Space

Day 50

Becoming Financially and Emotionally Wise

Wisdom grows through experience and reflection. As you continue your journey of healing and renewal, you may find yourself thinking more intentionally about how you manage both your emotions and your resources. Financial and emotional wisdom often develop together. When you become more aware of your needs, your boundaries, and your values, you begin to make choices that support stability and long-term peace.

Emotional wisdom allows you to respond thoughtfully rather than react impulsively. It encourages you to pause, reflect, and choose what aligns with your well-being. You begin to recognize what nurtures your peace and what disrupts it. This awareness helps you build stronger boundaries and healthier relationships. With emotional wisdom, you move through life with greater clarity and confidence.

Financial wisdom follows a similar path. It involves making thoughtful decisions about how you use and protect your resources. It means planning for stability, avoiding unnecessary strain, and honoring the value of what you have. Financial wisdom is not about having unlimited wealth. It is about using what you have with intention and care so that your life remains balanced and secure. Each wise decision contributes to a sense of independence and peace.

God cares about every area of your life, including your emotional and financial well-being. He desires for you to live with wisdom and stability.

When you seek His guidance, you gain clarity about the choices that support your growth and security. As Scripture reminds us, "If any of you lacks wisdom, you should ask God, who gives generously to all without finding fault, and it will be given to you." — James 1:5 (NIV). He helps you recognize what aligns with your values and what leads to lasting peace. With His support, you can move forward with confidence and thoughtful intention.

Today is an invitation to embrace wisdom in both your emotional and financial life. Consider what choices will support your stability and peace in the days ahead. Reflect on what you are learning about yourself and how you can use that knowledge to create a balanced future. Each step you take toward wise and intentional living strengthens your foundation and supports the life you are building.

Healing Reflection

What steps can you take to grow in emotional and financial wisdom so that your life feels more stable, balanced, and secure?

Reset Prayer

Gracious Father,

Thank You for guiding me toward wisdom and stability. Help me make thoughtful choices that support my emotional and financial well-being. Give me clarity in my decisions and discipline in my actions. Teach me to manage what I have with care and intention. Thank You for leading me toward a life that feels balanced, secure, and aligned with Your guidance. Amen.

Affirmation

I am becoming emotionally and financially wise. My choices support stability, growth, and lasting peace.

Your Reflection Space

Day 51

Walking in Discernment

Discernment is a quiet inner guidance that helps you recognize what is right for your life and what is not. It is the ability to sense when something brings peace and when something brings unease. As you continue to heal and grow, discernment becomes a valuable companion. It helps you make choices that protect your well-being and align with your values. Walking in discernment allows you to move forward with greater clarity and confidence.

There may have been times in the past when you overlooked your inner sense of knowing. You may have dismissed certain feelings or ignored gentle warnings because you hoped for a different outcome. With growth and reflection, you begin to recognize the importance of listening to that quiet inner voice. Discernment does not come from fear or suspicion. It comes from awareness, wisdom, and a desire for peace.

God offers guidance that strengthens your ability to discern. His presence brings clarity when situations feel confusing and calm when decisions feel overwhelming. When you take time to pause and reflect, you create space to sense what feels aligned with your well-being. Discernment often appears as a gentle awareness rather than a loud instruction. It may come as a sense of peace when something is right, confirming that you are aligned with wisdom and truth, or as a quiet hesitation when something is not, gently urging you to pause and reconsider.

As Scripture reminds us, "And this is my prayer: that your love may abound more and more in knowledge and depth of insight, so that you may be able to discern what is best..." — Philippians 1:9–10 (NIV)

Walking in discernment means trusting yourself enough to honor what you sense. It means permitting yourself to pause before making decisions and to consider what supports your peace and stability. You no longer feel pressured to say yes to everything or to follow paths that feel uncertain. Instead, you move with intention and awareness, choosing what nurtures your growth and protects your heart.

Today is an invitation to listen closely to your inner guidance. Notice how your body and mind respond to different situations and choices. Pay attention to what brings calm and what creates tension. Trust that you are developing the ability to discern what is best for your life. With practice and patience, discernment will become a steady and reliable guide as you continue moving forward.

Healing Reflection

Where in your life do you need greater discernment, and how can you begin trusting your inner sense of peace and clarity?

Reset Prayer

Wise and Loving Father,

Thank You for guiding me with wisdom and clarity. Help me walk in discernment and recognize what supports my peace and growth. Quiet the noise around me so I can hear Your gentle guidance. Give me the courage to trust what I sense and to make choices that align with my well-being. Thank You for leading me with patience and love as I continue this journey. Amen.

Affirmation

I walk in discernment and clarity. I trust the wisdom growing within me and choose what nurtures my peace.

Your Reflection Space

Protecting My New Peace

Peace that has been hard earned is something worth protecting. After walking through seasons of growth and healing, you may notice a new calm settling within your heart. This peace feels steady and reassuring. It allows you to breathe more freely and think more clearly. As this new sense of calm grows, you may also recognize the importance of guarding it with intention and care.

Protecting your peace does not require harshness or distance. It simply means being mindful of what you allow into your emotional and mental space. You begin to notice what nurtures your calm and what disrupts it. With this awareness, you make gentle choices that support your well-being. You may limit exposure to unnecessary stress, choose your conversations wisely, and create moments of quiet reflection that restore your spirit.

God desires for you to live in peace and stability. He understands the effort it has taken for you to reach this place of calm. As you move forward, His presence continues to guide and strengthen you. When you feel uncertain about what to allow or release, you can turn to Him for clarity. As Scripture reminds us, "Above all else, guard your heart, for everything you do flows from it." — Proverbs 4:23 (NIV) He gently reminds you that protecting your peace is not selfish. It is a wise and necessary part of living with balance and intention.

Protecting your new peace may involve setting boundaries, establishing healthy routines, or choosing environments that support your growth. These choices are acts of self-respect and awareness. Each time you honor your need for calm, you strengthen the foundation of your healing. Over time, this peace becomes a natural and steady part of your daily life.

Today is an invitation to recognize the peace that has begun to grow within you. Notice what helps it flourish and what threatens to disturb it. Commit to protecting this peace with kindness and wisdom. You have worked hard to reach this place of calm. It deserves to be nurtured and preserved. As you continue forward, your peace will remain a guiding force that supports your well-being and clarity.

Healing Reflection

What habits, boundaries, or choices will help you protect and maintain the peace you are building within your life?

Reset Prayer

Loving Father,
Thank You for the peace You are growing within my heart. Help me protect this peace with wisdom and care. Guide my choices so they reflect balance and calm. Give me the courage to step away from what disturbs my spirit and the strength to remain grounded in what nurtures me. Thank You for being my source of steady peace each day. Amen.

Affirmation

I protect my peace with wisdom and care. My calm and stability are valuable and worth preserving.

Your Reflection Space

Day 53

The Woman I Am Becoming

There is a quiet transformation taking place within you. With each day of healing, reflection, and growth, you are becoming a stronger and more grounded version of yourself. You may not notice every change as it happens, yet the woman you are becoming is shaped by every step you have taken. She is more aware, more peaceful, and more confident than before. She carries wisdom gained through experience and strength formed through perseverance.

You are no longer defined by past uncertainty or pain. You are defined by your willingness to grow and to move forward with intention. The woman you are becoming values her peace, honors her needs, and trusts her inner guidance. She understands that healing is not a destination but a continual unfolding. Each day offers another opportunity to live with clarity and purpose.

God sees the beauty of the transformation happening within you. He understands the journey that brought you here and the strength it required. With each step forward, He continues to guide and support you. As Scripture reminds us, "Being confident of this, that he who began a good work in you will carry it on to completion until the day of Christ Jesus." — Philippians 1:6 (NIV) The woman you are becoming reflects both grace and resilience. She is not rushed or pressured. She is growing at a pace that honors her healing and her well-being.

Becoming this woman does not require perfection. It requires presence and self-awareness. It means acknowledging your progress and treating yourself with kindness.

It means recognizing that you are evolving in meaningful ways. The strength you now carry is steady and grounded. The peace you feel is genuine and lasting. You are becoming someone who moves through life with confidence and calm.

Today is an invitation to honor the woman you are becoming. Reflect on the growth you have experienced and the clarity you now carry. Acknowledge your resilience and your capacity for renewal. You are not the same person you were at the beginning of this journey. You are stronger, wiser, and more at peace. Continue forward with confidence, knowing that your transformation is both real and lasting.

Healing Reflection

What qualities do you notice in the woman you are becoming, and how do these qualities reflect your growth and healing?

Reset Prayer

Gracious Father,
Thank You for the transformation taking place within me. Help me recognize the strength, wisdom, and peace that are growing in my life. Guide me as I continue becoming the woman You created me to be. Give me confidence in my journey and patience with my progress. Thank You for shaping my heart and leading me toward a life that reflects healing and purpose. Amen.

Affirmation

I honor the woman I am becoming. I am growing in strength, wisdom, and peace each day.

Your Reflection Space

Living Without Fear of Loss

Fear of loss can quietly shape the way you live. After experiencing disappointment, heartbreak, or unexpected change, it is natural to become cautious. You may guard your heart or hold back from fully embracing peace and joy because part of you fears that what you gain could one day be taken away. This quiet fear can create tension, making it difficult to feel secure even in moments of calm.

Living without fear of loss does not mean you will never face change. It means you choose not to let fear control how you experience the present. You begin to understand that peace and joy are meant to be lived fully, not held at a distance. You are allowed to enjoy stability, love, and calm without constantly preparing for them to disappear. Each moment of peace is a gift meant to be received with gratitude rather than fear.

God's presence offers a steady reassurance that goes beyond changing circumstances. Even when life shifts in unexpected ways, His care remains constant. As Scripture reminds us, "For I am convinced that neither death nor life, neither angels nor demons, neither the present nor the future, nor any powers... will be able to separate us from the love of God that is in Christ Jesus our Lord." — Romans 8:38–39 (NIV) When you trust that you are supported and guided, fear begins to lose its hold. You realize that your stability does not come solely from what surrounds you but from the strength and peace growing within you. With this understanding, you can live more freely and confidently.

Releasing the fear of loss is a gradual process. It begins with gentle awareness and a willingness to trust again. Each time you allow yourself to experience joy without hesitation, you weaken the hold of fear. Each time you focus on the present rather than worrying about what might happen, you strengthen your sense of peace. Over time, this practice creates a life that feels more open and grounded.

Today is an invitation to live fully in the present moment. Notice the peace and stability that exist in your life right now. Allow yourself to experience them without fear. You do not have to anticipate loss to protect yourself. You are supported, guided, and capable of navigating whatever comes. As you release fear, you make room for a deeper sense of freedom and calm to grow within you.

Healing Reflection

Where in your life have you been holding back out of fear of loss, and how can you begin to live more freely and fully in the present?

Reset Prayer

Faithful Father,
You know the fears that sometimes rise within me when I think about loss or change. Help me release these fears and trust in Your steady presence. Teach me to live fully in the peace and stability You provide. Strengthen my heart so I can embrace each day with confidence and gratitude. Thank You for guiding me and surrounding me with reassurance and care. Amen.

Affirmation

I release the fear of loss and embrace the peace of the present. I live with trust, freedom, and calm.

Your Reflection Space

Day 55

Trusting Myself Again

There may have been moments when you questioned your own judgment. After experiencing disappointment or emotional strain, it can be difficult to trust yourself fully. You may have wondered whether your choices were right or whether you overlooked something important. These thoughts can quietly weaken your confidence and make decision-making feel uncertain. Yet trusting yourself again is a natural part of healing and growth.

You have learned valuable lessons through every experience. Even the moments that felt confusing or painful have contributed to your wisdom. As you reflect on your journey, you begin to see that you are not the same person you were before. You have grown in awareness and understanding. You are more attuned to what supports your peace and what does not. This growth creates a strong foundation for renewed self-trust.

God has guided you through every step of your life, even when you felt unsure. His presence has helped shape your resilience and strengthen your insight. As Scripture reminds us, "Trust in the Lord with all your heart and lean not on your own understanding; in all your ways submit to him, and he will make your paths straight." — Proverbs 3:5–6 (NIV) As you continue forward, you can trust that the wisdom growing within you is supported by His guidance. You do not have to doubt every decision or second-guess your intuition. With faith and reflection, you can move forward with clarity and confidence.

Trusting yourself again begins with small steps. Listen to your inner voice when making choices.

Honor the feelings that signal what feels right or unsettled. Permit yourself to move forward without constant hesitation. Each time you trust your judgment and see positive results, your confidence deepens. Over time, this trust becomes steady and reliable.

Today is an invitation to reconnect with your inner sense of knowing. Recognize the growth and wisdom that now guide you. You are capable of making thoughtful and balanced decisions. You are able to choose what supports your peace and well-being. As you trust yourself again, you create a life that feels more grounded and secure.

Healing Reflection

Where in your life are you learning to trust your judgment again, and what signs show that your confidence is returning?

Reset Prayer

Loving Father,
Thank You for guiding me and helping me grow in wisdom. Help me trust the insight and understanding that are developing within me. Remove doubt and replace it with clarity and confidence. Guide my decisions so they align with peace and purpose. Thank You for helping me trust myself again as I continue moving forward. Amen.

Affirmation

I trust myself again. My wisdom is growing, and my decisions are guided by clarity and peace.

Your Reflection Space

God Is Doing a New Thing in Me

There are seasons in life when you can feel a quiet shift taking place within your heart. You may notice new thoughts forming, new strength rising, and a deeper sense of peace settling into your spirit. These changes may not always be dramatic, yet they are meaningful. They are signs that something new is unfolding within you. Growth often begins quietly before it becomes fully visible.

You are not the same person you were at the beginning of this journey. The experiences you have faced and the healing you have embraced have created space for renewal. Old patterns and heavy emotions are slowly being replaced with clarity and calm. Where there was once uncertainty, you may now sense a growing confidence. Where there was once pain, you may now feel the beginnings of peace. These changes reflect the new work taking place within you.

God is always at work, even when the changes feel subtle. As Scripture reminds us, "See, I am doing a new thing! Now it springs up; do you not perceive it?" — Isaiah 43:19 (NIV). He understands your journey and the transformation happening in your heart. His presence brings renewal and guidance, helping you move forward with strength and purpose. When you allow yourself to trust this process, you begin to see that each step you take is leading you toward a life that feels more balanced and fulfilling.

Embracing what is new within you requires openness and patience. You may not fully understand every change, and that is perfectly acceptable. Growth does not always follow a clear or predictable path. It unfolds gently, one step at a time. As you continue to trust and move forward, you will notice that the new strength and peace within you become steadier and more familiar.

Today is an invitation to acknowledge the transformation taking place in your life. Notice the ways you are thinking, feeling, and responding differently. Celebrate the growth that is quietly unfolding within you. God is doing a new thing in you, shaping your heart and guiding your path. Allow yourself to move forward with hope and trust, knowing that each new step is leading you toward greater peace and purpose.

Healing Reflection

What new thoughts, habits, or feelings have you noticed within yourself that show growth and renewal are taking place?

Reset Prayer

Faithful Father,

Thank You for the new work You are doing within me. Help me recognize the growth and renewal taking place in my life. Give me patience and trust as I continue to change and grow. Strengthen my heart and guide my steps toward peace and purpose. Thank You for leading me into a new season filled with clarity and hope. Amen.

Affirmation

God is doing a new thing in me. I welcome growth, renewal, and the peace that comes with transformation.

Your Reflection Space

My Future Is Still Beautiful

There may have been moments when you wondered what the future would hold for you. After walking through seasons of pain, uncertainty, or unexpected change, it is natural to question what lies ahead. You may have felt as though certain dreams were delayed or that parts of your life did not unfold as you once hoped. Yet your future is not defined by what has already happened. It is still filled with possibility, growth, and beauty waiting to unfold.

Your life continues to move forward with purpose. Each day carries new opportunities for peace, stability, and fulfillment. Even if the path looks different from what you once imagined, it can still lead to meaningful and joyful experiences. The wisdom you have gained through your journey has prepared you for what lies ahead. You now carry a deeper awareness of your needs, your values, and your strength. These qualities will guide you toward a future that feels steady and fulfilling.

God sees the fullness of your journey and the potential that still lies before you. He understands the hopes within your heart and the peace you seek. As Scripture reminds us, "For I know the plans I have for you," declares the Lord, "plans to prosper you and not to harm you, plans to give you hope and a future." — Jeremiah 29:11 (NIV) His guidance does not end with past challenges. It continues into every new chapter of your life. When you trust that your future remains open and filled with promise, you allow yourself to move forward with renewed hope. You begin to see possibilities where you once saw limitations.

Believing that your future is still beautiful requires gentle faith. It asks you to release the idea that your best days are behind you. It invites you to imagine a life that continues to grow in peace and purpose. Each step you take now contributes to the life you are building. With patience and trust, you will see beauty emerge in ways you may not have expected.

Today is an invitation to look ahead with hope rather than hesitation. Consider what you want your future to feel like. Imagine a life filled with calm, stability, and meaningful moments. Allow yourself to believe that such a future is possible. Your journey is not ending. It is unfolding. The beauty that lies ahead is shaped by the strength and growth you carry within you.

Healing Reflection

When you think about your future, what hopes or peaceful possibilities do you want to believe are still waiting for you?

Reset Prayer

Loving Father,
Thank You for the future that still lies before me. Help me release any fear or doubt about what is ahead. Fill my heart with hope and confidence as I move forward. Guide my steps toward peace, stability, and purpose. Remind me that my life continues to unfold with beauty and meaning. Thank You for walking with me into every new chapter. Amen.

Affirmation

My future is still beautiful. I move forward with hope, peace, and confidence in what lies ahead.

Your Reflection Space

Day 58

I Choose Peace Daily

Peace is not always something that simply appears. Often it is something you choose, moment by moment and day by day. Life can bring unexpected situations, strong emotions, and moments of uncertainty. In the midst of all these experiences, peace becomes a steady anchor that helps you remain grounded. Choosing peace is an intentional decision to respond with calm and clarity rather than stress or fear.

You may have spent time reacting to circumstances in ways that left you feeling unsettled. Over time, you have learned that your inner peace is valuable and worth protecting. Choosing peace daily means being mindful of your thoughts, your words, and your surroundings. It means pausing before reacting and asking yourself what response will bring calm rather than tension. Each time you make that choice, you strengthen your sense of balance.

God's presence offers a constant source of peace that you can draw from each day. As Scripture reminds us, "You will keep in perfect peace those whose minds are steadfast, because they trust in you." — Isaiah 26:3 (NIV) When you feel overwhelmed or uncertain, you can pause and reconnect with that steady presence. His peace does not depend on perfect circumstances. It remains available even when life feels unpredictable. As you turn toward Him, you find reassurance and calm that guide your responses and decisions.

Choosing peace daily may involve setting boundaries, creating quiet moments, or gently redirecting your thoughts. These choices do not remove all challenges, but they change how you experience them.

Instead of feeling consumed by stress, you begin to move through situations with greater steadiness. Over time, peace becomes a natural part of how you live rather than something you must search for.

Today is an opportunity to affirm your commitment to peace. Notice where you can choose calm instead of worry and patience instead of frustration. Each peaceful decision strengthens your sense of stability and well-being. You are creating a life where peace is not occasional but consistent. With intention and trust, you continue to move forward with a calm and centered heart.

Healing Reflection

What daily choices or habits can help you maintain a sense of peace and calm in your thoughts and actions?

Reset Prayer

Gracious Father,
Thank You for the peace that is always available to me. Help me choose calm and clarity in every situation I face. Guide my thoughts and responses so they reflect wisdom and balance. When I feel overwhelmed, remind me to pause and return to Your presence. Thank You for filling my heart with peace that steadies me each day. Amen.

Affirmation

I choose peace each day. My heart is calm, centered, and guided by clarity and faith.

Your Reflection Space

Day 59

I Have Survived, and I Am Still Rising

There are chapters of your life that require more strength than you ever imagined you had. Moments when you felt stretched beyond comfort, when uncertainty seemed overwhelming, and when you wondered how you would move forward. Yet you did move forward. You endured what once felt unbearable. You stood through seasons that tried to shake your stability. Today you can look back and recognize a powerful truth. You have survived.

Surviving is not a small achievement. It reflects resilience, courage, and a determination that remained even in your most difficult moments. There were days when simply continuing was an act of strength. There were moments when hope felt distant, yet something within you continued to rise. That inner strength has carried you through every challenge and brought you to where you stand today.

Rising is the next part of your journey. It means you are no longer only surviving what has happened. You are growing beyond it. Each day you stand with renewed clarity and peace, you rise a little higher. You move with greater awareness of your worth and your purpose. As Scripture reminds us, "But those who hope in the Lord will renew their strength. They will soar on wings like eagles; they will run and not grow weary, they will walk and not be faint." — Isaiah 40:31 (NIV) Rising does not require perfection. It simply asks that you continue forward with faith in your own strength and the support that surrounds you.

God has been with you through every season of your life. He has seen your tears, your questions, and your perseverance. Even in moments when you felt alone, His presence remained steady. Now, as you rise into a new season, He continues to guide you with compassion and care. Your story is not one of defeat. It is a story of resilience and renewal.

Today is an invitation to honor the strength that has carried you this far. Reflect on what you have overcome and how you continue to grow. You are not defined by what you endured. You are defined by the strength that allowed you to rise again. Your journey reflects courage, and your future holds continued growth and peace. You have survived, and you are still rising with grace and strength.

Healing Reflection

What challenges have you survived that now reveal the strength and resilience you carry within you today?

Reset Prayer

Faithful Father,
Thank You for sustaining me through every challenge and guiding me through every season. Help me honor the strength You have built within me. Remind me that I am not defined by my struggles but by the resilience and growth that continue to shape my life. Give me courage to keep rising and faith to move forward with hope. Thank You for walking beside me and lifting me into new seasons of peace and strength. Amen.

Affirmation

I have survived and I am still rising. My strength, resilience, and hope continue to carry me forward.

Your Reflection Space

Day 60

From Broken to Becoming

This journey began with honesty about pain and the quiet acknowledgment of what your heart had been carrying. There were moments when you felt fragile, uncertain, and in need of restoration. You allowed yourself to face those feelings with courage and openness. Day by day, you chose healing. Step by step, you moved forward. Today, you stand in a new place, not defined by what once broke you, but by who you are becoming.

Becoming is a process filled with growth and renewal. It reflects the strength that rises after hardship and the peace that follows reflection. You are no longer standing in the same emotional space where this journey began. Your perspective has shifted. Your heart has softened and strengthened at the same time. You have learned to honor your needs, protect your peace, and trust your inner wisdom. These changes mark the beautiful transformation taking place within you.

Being broken was never your final state. It was a season that invited reflection and healing. Becoming is the continuation of your story. As Scripture reminds us, "We all, who with unveiled faces contemplate the Lord's glory, are being transformed into his image with ever-increasing glory, which comes from the Lord, who is the Spirit." — 2 Corinthians 3:18 (NIV) It is the unfolding of a life that feels more balanced, peaceful, and aligned with your true self. Each lesson you have learned and each step you have taken have contributed to this moment. You carry forward wisdom, resilience, and a deeper understanding of your own worth.

God has walked with you through every part of this journey. He has seen your tears and your courage.

He has strengthened you in moments when you felt uncertain and guided you toward peace when you needed it most. As you continue forward, His presence remains steady. The woman you are becoming reflects grace, strength, and quiet confidence. You are moving into a life that feels more grounded and hopeful.

Today is a moment to pause and honor your transformation. Reflect on how far you have come and the growth that has taken place within you. You have moved from brokenness into becoming. You have chosen healing, peace, and renewal. This journey does not end here. It continues with each new day and each new choice you make. Carry forward the strength and clarity you have gained. You are becoming a woman who lives with purpose, peace, and confidence in what lies ahead.

Healing Reflection

As you complete this journey, what changes do you see within yourself, and what intentions do you carry forward into the next chapter of your life?

Reset Prayer

Gracious Father,

Thank You for walking with me through every step of this journey. Thank You for healing my heart and guiding me from brokenness into becoming. Help me carry forward the peace, wisdom, and strength I have gained. Continue shaping my life with purpose and clarity. Remind me that I am still growing and still becoming. Thank You for Your steady presence and for the new season unfolding before me. Amen.

Affirmation

I have moved from broken to becoming. I walk forward with peace, strength, and confidence in who I am becoming.

YOUR REFLECTION SPACE

Closing Blessing

As you reach the end of this journey, take a quiet moment to acknowledge how far you have come.

You began these pages carrying memories, questions, and emotions that needed space to be seen and understood. Along the way, you allowed yourself to reflect, release, and grow. You chose healing in moments when it would have been easier to remain guarded. You chose peace when old patterns invited you back into tension. You chose to move forward, one honest step at a time.

May the clarity you have gained remain with you.
May the peace you have cultivated continue to steady your heart.
May the strength you discovered in difficult seasons guide you through every new chapter ahead.

As you move forward, trust your growth and honor your needs. Protect the calm you have worked to build and welcome the joy returning to your life. Let the wisdom you now carry shape your decisions and strengthen your confidence.

Remember that healing is not a single destination but an ongoing unfolding. There will be new lessons, new beginnings, and new growth opportunities. You are prepared for them. You carry resilience, awareness, and the ability to begin again whenever necessary.
May your days be filled with calm, your thoughts with clarity, and your future with quiet hope.

May you continue to grow into the woman you are becoming, steady, self-aware, and at peace. And may you always move forward knowing that your life is still unfolding in meaningful and beautiful ways.

Final Reflection

Take a quiet moment and reflect on how far you have come.

What has shifted within your heart?

What have you released, and what strength have you discovered?

Honor your growth. Acknowledge your healing.

Write freely and honestly in this space.

This moment belongs to you.

ABOUT THE AUTHOR

Charma-Lee Ritchie is a faith-driven author and creator devoted to helping individuals and families heal, grow, and rediscover their identity through God. Her work speaks to the silent struggles many carry, offering truth, restoration, and spiritual clarity through every page.

Through her writing, she creates space for reflection, renewal, and transformation, guiding readers from brokenness into becoming. Her books span devotionals and inspirational works for women, men, and children, each designed to meet readers where they are and lead them forward with purpose.

Her mission is simple yet powerful: to help others release what weighs them down, embrace truth, and walk boldly in who God has called them to be.

CONTINUE YOUR HEALING JOURNEY

SPIRITUAL GROWTH & PRAYER

Urgent Prayers
A Spirit-Led Guide to Breakthrough in Every Area of Life

Prayer Journal for Women: 64 Week Guided Prayer, Scripture, &
Devotional
Prayer Journal for Men: A daily Christian Journal for men to strengthen
your faith - with encouraging Bible verses to build your confidence

CREATIVE & REFLECTIVE

My Magical Garden Coloring Book
A Creative Journey of Calm and Reflection
Girl, You Are Beautiful Coloring Book
Affirmations and Creative Inspiration

CHILDREN'S BOOKS

Mindfulness Journal for Kids - A Growth Mindset Guided Journal for
Children Aged 7-12 to help Reduce Anxiety & Stay Happy & Calm

Richard Wants a Moon
Richard's Changing Tree
Lila and the Stars and More
Stay connected and access more resources: Visit
www.charmaleeritchie.com